ARTICULAT

On The Utilisatic
and Meanings of Psyc

Articulations: On the Utilisation and Meanings of Psychedelics

by Julian Palmer

Copyright © 2014-2015 by Julian Palmer

Published by Anastomosis Books

Cover and Book Design: Antonia Green: antgreen33@gmail.com

Illustrations: Matt Wilson: dream@pariah66.com

Proofreading and Editorial Advice: Jenji San, Jonathon Hale and Sophie Hawkes

ISBN: 978-0-9925528-0-0

Dewey Number: 154.4

Subjects: Psychotropic drugs–Therapeutic use–Effectiveness.
Psychotropic plants–Therapeutic use–Effectiveness. Mental healing.
Psychopharmacology–Research.

Third Edition

Printed by Ingram Spark

http://www.julianpalmerism.com

ARTICULATIONS

On The Utilisation
and Meanings of Psychedelics

by

Julian Palmer

Contents

Preface

Articulations is a written effort to comprehend the meaning of psychedelic states, how these states can be practically interpreted, and ultimately how we can effectively and intelligently utilise these psychedelic plants and compounds. Science, as the essential religion of the times, is not an authoritative reference point for this work, as there is relatively little that modern-day science can communicate, or has communicated, regarding the subjectively complex world of interior psychedelic states. That being said, I do hope that much of what I have shared here can be an inspiration for scientists and researchers of all kinds, to allow further understanding of these states of consciousness.

In this work, I have reported my observations, understandings and what many would consider to be 'theories'. This type of thoughtfulness and reflection, I believe, can be useful for decoding the most basic elements of the psychedelic state and allow an acute focus on the various cultural issues associated with psychedelics. I have no doubt that these perceptions accurately reflect the actualities of people's experiences of these states. While I understand that many will see these understandings and views as quite 'far out', I think that if we are to advance human understanding, our foundational premises must evolve and transform to reflect the actualities of human experience. Much of what is written here is of a philosophic bent and is meant to be, 'true enough!' as the American psychedelic philosopher Terence McKenna would say. In that light, I have attempted to formally, colorfully, and contextually address the many aspects of the psychedelic experience, so that the layperson or experienced psychedelic explorer can more easily understand and decipher what actually occurs for them in the psychedelic state.

I do believe the present Western models of understanding and most of the maps available, even those of eastern mysticism, quantum physics, or any form of shamanism, do not provide enough scope to truly understand the psychedelic phenomenon on its own terms. So this book is not a map, but perhaps more of a travel guide, into which a great deal of practical research has been carried out.

I also believe that within this book I am communicating on behalf of the thousands of people I have spoken with regarding their experiences, and many of these words could easily be theirs as much as mine. For those new to this area, if they desire to have such experiences themselves, there are some guidelines or ideas about how to safely and consciously commence this exploration.

It has been commonly said in the past that 'knowledge is power', yet in this age of Google, information ceases to represent a real power, when so much information is at most people's fingertips. Yet, the ability to be inspired and 'do something' with information is where a more essential power lies. Many read and type, but few act, especially when it comes to psychedelics, highlighting the often extreme fear and reticence many have toward these states. This book is not a clarion call to take psychedelics, but a sounding board for those who already engage with psychedelics or for those who may want to take their first steps.

This book arose out of 15 years of deep immersion into the world of psychedelics. There are very few people in this world that I have met, if any, who have had the extensive experience I have had with ayahuasca, the many DMT-containing plants, and also synthetic compounds like the phenethylamines, ketamine, 5-MeO-DMT, as well as other psychedelic plants such as iboga, to be able to make assessments about these materials, how they work, and how we can use them. During over thousands of hours of 'flight time', I came to understand not only these compounds, but I also gained some unique perceptions regarding the nature of human life itself. My own investigations were ambitious and I sought not answers, but results. I was enmeshed in revealing meaning, involved in processes of healing and collective transformation. I suppose I undertook a kind of education, but also went through many trials and ordeals, in both the inner and outer world. This work emerges from many years of being subjected to forces and pressures that have stimulated and shaped me.

This book does not aim to share technical knowledge about psychoactive chemicals and plants. These days such information can easily be found on the internet or in many other books. What I stress in this work is a primary issue: that the use of psychedelics for the purpose of increasing self under-standing, personal growth, and both emotional and mental awareness, can assist individuals to realise how to cause less pain to themselves and other human beings, and optimise their ability to create true and lasting fulfil-ment in themselves and others. I believe that these plants and substances can be extremely beneficial and useful, but may also present many potential pitfalls and troubles. With broadminded knowledge and understanding of how these psychedelics work, we can utilise these tools with a constructive mindset. Thus this book was born.

Chapter One

The Revelation of DMT

First Steps

The first time I tried to have a breakthrough experience by smoking crystal DMT (N,N-Dimethyltryptamine), I wasn't able to inhale enough of the harsh smoke and had a gentle kind of experience in which some colourful, but indistinct beings, telepathically communicated to me, "You really don't need this. Live your life, as it is what you truly have. We have – ALL THIS. But, what is most important is your life and how you live it!"

When I had refined my smoking technique and was finally able to truly break through, I went out of my body into a phantasmagorical world, where I was shown marvelous forms of being and felt completely safe and loved. I was exhilarated by the experience and had many more breakthrough experiences over the next few months, going even deeper into the indescribable.

In those days, the DMT smoke from the waxy, red *Acacia obtusifolia* crystal was like nectar to me. I could easily smoke over a point, or 100mg, quite a strong dose, in one big lung hit through a glass crack pipe. But it wasn't always easy. Before smoking the DMT, I would often pace around and fret for up to two hours and typically listen to a CD of electronic chill music called 'Goa Transcendental' on repeat. Now, I have no fear or even anxiety regarding smoking DMT. After spending a long time working through it,

I eventually realised deep in my being, that there's simply no purpose to such anxiety or fear.

Even over 15 years later, I still have flashes of what I experienced in those days. These adventures changed my life. I knew for sure that 'something else' existed apart from the physical realm, because I had experienced it. This 'something else' completely revealed its nature – not that I could ever totally understand it. However, I knew firsthand that whatever was beyond the physical realm was extraordinarily intelligent and sophisticated. These experiences infused my being with a sense of trust and some sort of direct understanding of the continuum of life.

I was never able to truly remember the most impressive states I would enter. It seemed that going 'there' was so beyond the ken of the human brain's normal operation, that there was no way the everyday brain state could remember, contain, or even truly reference what had happened. However, when I smoked DMT again and entered into that expanded state, I would remember all my other DMT experiences.

The effect that smoking DMT had on my consciousness was that I gained a direct understanding that inside us or beyond us are worlds of quantum multidimensionality far beyond this one. Sometimes, the experiences showed me worlds of being more real than this world. What I experienced was beyond any 'Disneyworld' because it was real. At times, if I did doubt or had difficulty in accepting what was happening, I would be told to wake up and get with it. These experiences eventually brought me to become more committed to life in this world, rather than seeking other worlds or answers in the beyond. I learned that I needed to appreciate the human experience for what it is, having truly peeked beyond the veils of this 'illusion'.

Smoking Crystal DMT

When crystal DMT is smoked or vaporised it gives the individual an experience that may last from a few minutes to a quarter of an hour. DMT has traditionally been vaporised through a glass crack pipe, which is quite an effective smoking method if carried out properly – although the smoke is quite harsh and it takes some skill to be able to smoke the DMT quickly enough for this technique to be truly effective. The trick to using a glass pipe is to smoke as much DMT as you can, as quickly as you can, preferably in one long hit, while not going into a coughing fit. Before smoking DMT it is advisable to first open up the lungs by doing some deep breathing exercises, in which you must breathe in as much as you can and breathe out as much as you can, in order to open up and prepare your lungs. It is also a good idea to massage your chest and thymus area (along the centre of the breastbone in line with the shoulder joints) while breathing deeply for a few minutes until you are fully oxygenated. Then light your pipe as you are over half way through breathing out, and when you have fully expelled the air out of your lungs, you can begin to slowly sip in the smoke. The trick here is not to vaporise the DMT too quickly because then you will be taking in too much of the harsh smoke all at once, which will likely result in a coughing fit.

You will want to slowly caress the DMT out of the bottom of the pipe and swirl the lighter (a jet-flame or normal lighter) around the DMT so it vaporises consistently. You will get to a point when you have smoked over two-thirds of your DMT in one long slow toke, and at that point you will begin to feel lift off. A short, compact inhalation is imperative here, as the quicker you can get the smoke down into your lungs, the further you will go.

The trick to most effectively smoking DMT is to pull the smoke down through the throat into the bottom of your lungs. At some point while inhaling the smoke, your lungs may protest as the smoke is very harsh. DMT tastes and feels like burnt plastic. When you have pulled as much smoke as you can into your lungs, ideally until there is no more left, or when you simply cannot inhale anymore, hold the smoke in for as long as you can. Then you may likely feel your lungs beginning to melt, and at this point, you will often not even feel the need for breathing. Now, breathe out the smoke through your nose in one exhalation, as doing so appears to facilitate a deeper visionary experience. This is perhaps the trickiest way to smoke DMT, but it is far from being the best way, and I wouldn't actually recommend it to people as the best way to smoke DMT.

The simplest and most accessible way to smoke freebase crystal DMT is with some herbs through a bong or some sort of water pipe. Good herbs to use include *Banisteriopsis caapi* (ayahuasca) leaf or vine, passionflower, peppermint, mullein, or even parsley. The trick is to load the cone with a little bit of herb, then put the DMT on top, and then add some more herbs so that the DMT is sandwiched in between two layers of herb. It is important to make sure that the lighter flame does not make direct contact with the DMT, as that will burn the DMT at too high a temperature and perhaps negatively affect the experience. The bong can then be smoked like any bong is smoked, and the whole package ideally taken into the lungs in one long and consistent pull.

50mg to 100 mg of DMT is a good, standard amount to smoke, as any less will not tend to catalyse a deep and profound breakthrough experience. Some rare individuals will need up to about 200 mg of DMT in order to truly 'break through'. These days, some people are beginning to use hand-held vaporiser devices like a vapor genie, or even e-cigarettes in order to smoke DMT, and those who use them will often swear you could never go back to smoking DMT any other way. However, I'm yet to be convinced and think that a water bong is the most immediate and direct way to smoke DMT for most people.

Changa (DMT infused into a combination of various herbs, typically including ayahuasca leaf or vine) can be used to have breakthrough DMT experiences as well. Although changa typically produces sub-breakthrough experiences in which the smoker stays in the realm of the body, yet still has visions and experiences of a profound nature. I have heard of people smoking one changa joint containing 25% DMT in a quick smoking session, to have profound breakthrough experiences. But normally a pipe, or even better, a bong is used for breakthrough DMT experiences. If the DMT content of the changa is a light blend of 20 – 25% , it might take two or three good cones, taken in succession to break through. Or, if the changa is 40 - 50% DMT, then it should take one full-sized cone or two smaller cones smoked within 30 seconds to really break through. Smoking changa like this is a very effective and quite easy way to have a breakthrough DMT experience.

So how do you know when you really 'break through'? Well, for one thing, there is no amount of DMT that will guarantee a breakthrough experience. Some people may smoke very large amounts of DMT and still remain within the limits of their mind and body. The breakthrough is generally considered to be an experience that is beyond the boundaries of the mind and body, and is therefore quite similar to an out-of-body experience. The experience involves engaging with the profound and the typically indescribable. If you are still in your body, looking at beings, or have some semblance of your mind and your body, then the experience could still technically be called 'sub-breakthrough'. The breakthrough experience requires that the individual smokes quite a large amount of DMT, something not always that easy to do. People talk about going beyond 'the dome' and the different levels and gates you can get to, which often seem to be quite a number. What is revealed during the DMT experience is likely to be very different for each person. For myself, smoking DMT has involved engaging in absolutely shocking realities, and these are the sort of experience that some may only be inclined to have once in their life.

You know you have smoked too much DMT when you don't remember a thing and there are signs of 'overdose'. There may be convulsions – not serious full body shaking, but involving some shaking and shuddering. There may be frothing at the mouth. The eyes may move around in an alien way. Some people's eyes might roll back into their head and there may be vomiting. Having said this, what may be very perturbing for onlookers can often be overwhelmingly positive for the person having these experiences. They may be having powerful 'out of body' experiences in other realms of being. People who have smoked DMT many times and given it to dozens, if not hundreds of people, will tell you that the fantastic and extremely meaningful nature of other dimensions is what people normally report in a breakthrough experience. What the other dimensions look like is not quite possible to explain, as they are very different from the three-dimensional world we know. A world of four or five or six dimensions cannot be described or even truly comprehended when we are back in three dimensions. However, it is useful to know that these other dimensions exist. What we can actually do with this knowledge in the three-dimensional world is however another matter.

By smoking DMT, people do often see very sophisticated landscapes and beings. In other words, they come across forms of sentience and the environments in which that sentience resides. If we are to think about it, what else could there be that we could experience? What else is there, in fact, that could exist in other dimensions? It is also common for people to experience states of consciousness that the mystics have traditionally described, such as pure emptiness, or experiencing states of transcendent unity with the earth, the universe and universal beingness.

For those who have experienced these states of being, it is very much like seeing that the world is in fact round, not flat. The North American philosopher Ken Wilber calls a worldview without spirit 'flatland'. For most who have seen the realms of the spirit world there is normally no doubt, no question of the existence of this realm – of an existence beyond the brain, beyond the body. That the world is round is not something that can be entirely accepted on faith, but the good news is that pretty much anyone can discover the new world and see for themselves. There are some who say they have smoked DMT and then state they don't believe what they experience is 'real'. But what is real? This question represents one of the most enduring philosophical tail chases human beings know.

When discussing what type of experiences people have after smoking DMT, there are a few factors to consider first. For DMT to be truly effective you must smoke a great deal of it, and that is often quite tricky to do. Secondly, it is often the case that some of the DMT in any given country is synthetic. Reports from synthetic DMT vary. Some people say it can be very strong and powerful and others say it isn't comparable to natural DMT and only gives a caricature of an experience.

Also, we must take into account the character of the person smoking DMT. Fellow explorers have noticed that particularly unpleasant people often have particularly unpleasant experiences. I heard of a man who had basically tried to rape a friend of his, who ended up being raped by a reptilian creature and then flung far into the cosmos. After that experience he apparently didn't speak more than a few words at a time for two weeks. I was also told of two men who approached DMT in a particularly gung-ho and insensitive way. Both of them experienced their faces opening up like drawbridges – and then both witnessed a vigilante gang armed with torches, pitchforks and miscellaneous weapons going into their mouths to attack the brain of each man. At the end of this rattling experience, the drawbridge opened up again and the crowd poured back out through mouth of them both. I was also told about another man with a known inability to look at himself, who used to take out his particularly damaged nature on other people, who experienced himself in an ambulance dying for the entire duration of his experience. These experiences share a common factor – there is no content provided in the experience, only a kind of disapproval and even punishment, which seems to accord with how these people treat reality. 'You reap what you sow.'

There are those who do fear DMT, and we could not accurately talk about DMT, without mentioning that many people simply do find it horrifying. The more juicy beings and environments, especially those that are more so-phisticated and startling, do not simply show up to everyone. It is perhaps only something like 20% of people who smoke DMT who report seeing these very startling beings the first time they smoke DMT. There are also realms of lower order beings who are comparatively '8 bit', and much that is revealed by DMT can at times be underwhelming, repetitive and even boring. This contrasts with the extremely startling and mind-blowing experiences that have nothing on the closing scenes of the science fiction film *2001: A Space Odyssey*. Furthermore, these mind blowing experiences do not necessarily arise on demand, just because you decide to smoke a potent neurotransmitter. It is possible to have many experiences of an extraordinary magnitude, but you can just as often have experiences that are much less impressive and even quite flimsy.

How people respond to their DMT experiences varies immensely, but many people use the words 'life changing'. And yet, some people do not appear to be changed in any significant way by DMT. It seems that there must be a certain degree of ability to contextualise the experience within the indi-vidual. When it comes to interpreting the breakthrough experience, there is often no way it can be easily contextualised, only some awareness of what has occurred. It is very clear to many that the magnitude and meaningfulness of the DMT experience can make it quite difficult for many who encounter it, to say these experiences are simply artifacts of the functioning of the 'brain'. Some say that the states of being generated by DMT represent dreaming while awake; yet the DMT state is typically very different from the most common dream state of experiencing unusual stories from an assumed 1st person perspective. It is not uncommon for people to report being given a pipe of DMT within a dream and these 'DMT experiences' are said to be the most powerful and interesting of all. Of course, these sorts of reports give us something of an understanding of the power of the human brain and consciousness.

By smoking DMT, we can directly discover and understand the ineffable nature of consciousness, a consciousness that reveals itself to exist beyond the brain, yet is focused through the brain, body and nervous system. In many respects, profound DMT experiences can be very liberating to individuals. Importantly, DMT can allow people to look deeply into the fear of death, one of the most stubborn and enduring issues that individuals face. When it is directly realised that consciousness is in fact not just the body, many are able to release the fear of death. This fear appears to exist because of exclusive identification with the physical body and the physical domain as the only form of true life, which is actually not the case, assuming we accept there are other domains of existence apart from the purely physical.

The Canadian actor Jim Carrey once talked of a classic mystical experience that was said to be induced by meditation, but is an experience that many DMT smokers can resonate with:

> "I suddenly felt I was looking at these thoughts from another perspective and I wondered, who is it that's aware that I am thinking? And suddenly I was thrown into this expansive, amazing feeling of freedom – from myself, from my problems, I saw that I was bigger than what I do, I was bigger than my body, I was everything and everyone. I was no longer a fragment of the universe, I was the universe and ever since that day I've been trying to get back there. It comes and it goes. Sometimes it's like riding a wave, sometimes I'm on, sometimes I'm

off. But at least I know where I want to go and I want to take as many people as I possibly can because the feeling is amazing."

The Hindu perspective is that the world is a form of illusion, a kind of dream they call 'maya'. In the DMT state, you are not dreaming within the dream, rather you are waking up from the dream, to the extent that you can. It may not be useful to continue to chase this sort of experience throughout one's life. That is why high doses of DMT often ceases to continue to be effective, because the message is such a simple one. Once the human being receives the message, it seems that there are only so many times it can be received, and there is also the sense that too much information will spoil your human experience. Quite a few friends describe encountering beings asking, "Why are you back here? Haven't we already told you everything?"

I know a fellow who says that such beings are gatekeepers and you must move past them to go deeper into other realms. He claims that if you keep pushing, you can go deeper into other realms of liquid blue light and so on. Personally, I have found that if I keep pushing, the experiences can become 'dark' and you can meet all kinds of crazy semi-malevolent beings. Many people are quite spiritually ambitious, and I think DMT can show us how unnecessary this type of ambition is.

Rational Interpretations

Modern rationalists typically see the existence of spirits or other beings as an irrational phenomenon, a return to a prerational state.

As Ken Wilber says in his book *Sex, Ecology and Spirituality*:

> "In these reductionist accounts, rationality is the great and final omega point of individual and collective development, the high-water mark of all evolution. No deeper or wider or higher context is thought to exist. Thus, life is to be lived either rationally, or neurotically (Freud's concept of neurosis is basically anything that derails the emergence of rational

perception – true enough as far as it goes, which is just not all that far). Since no higher context is thought to be real, or to actually exist, then whenever any genuinely transrational occasion occurs, it is immediately explained as a regression to prerational structures (since they are the only nonrational structures allowed, and thus the only ones to accept an explanatory hypothesis). The superconscious is reduced to the subconscious, the transpersonal is collapsed to the prepersonal, and the emergence of the higher is reinterpreted as an eruption from the lower. All breathe a sigh of relief, and the rational world space is not fundamentally shaken (by 'the black tide of the mud of occultism!' as Freud so quaintly explained it to Jung)."

Yet, who decides what is prerational and what is transrational? Spirits are reported in most of the world's shamanic traditions and religions. Perhaps the word 'superconsciousness' presupposes some sort of pinnacle of consciousness, whereas for the shaman, communicating with spirits is part of his or her day-to-day work. My experience of spirits is that they didn't look like Casper the ghost, all wispy and transparent. They rocked my world. They came in and did operations on me. They shape-shifted into many different forms that typically far exceeded any of our known human art in beauty. The technology they showed me was far beyond any technology we have on earth. Meetings with these beings left me in a state of awe and wonder.

However, it took some time and many, many encounters with these beings until my rational mind could no longer deny that what I was experiencing was what it appeared to be. That is, the spirits were actually as they said they were – independent beings from another dimension or realm of existence. Some of them would visit to provide support. Sometimes they did not communicate much, but I could see them and their apparent clothes that radiated a sense of their own inner self and commanded great respect. In all of this, there was a sense of profound technology, and a level of advancement far beyond the human. Sometimes these beings were huge, and sometimes they were quite small or didn't seem to have a size at all.

Other times the spirits were there just to entertain me. They were solid and radiant. Often, they emanated colours that do not exist in the human world. To label this vast phenomena with the word 'spirits' or 'beings' seemed quite ridiculous to me. I did not go around telling people of these visitations, because they were continual. Sometimes in one ayahuasca session, I would meet dozens and dozens of these beings and they would often communicate and try to teach me things. It is absolutely inconceivable to me that these beings could be emanations of my brain, as they were so obviously alien. Yet these beings often did say, "I am you. We are you." But it was not that they communicated they were a part of my 'mind' (as I knew it), but of a much larger and inclusive network of consciousness. And when they departed, they always gracefully receded into the great beyond from where they came.

Many people who read the reports of people smoking DMT, might feel such reports seem too fantastic to be at all credible. But what does credible even mean? Even those who have these experiences often do not believe they are having them. A typical DMT experience may involve the individual continually feeling disbelief, while the mysterious other ramps up the stakes, until there is only surrender.

I think that what appears as miraculous or magical to us is, in fact, only more advanced forms of what we can understand as technology. In the DMT state, we are the indigenous tribal villagers being bamboozled by the phonographs and photographs that the interstellar missionaries are showing us. They will often show us these very advanced technologies, which our relatively primitive mind will interpret as magic. Although, as the science fiction writer Arthur C. Clarke put it, "Magic is just science that we don't understand yet."

The magical and miraculous are then not fantasies, but actually represent a vaster understanding of how reality can be engineered. The nature of the universe in its evolution only expands its potential for the engineering of different forms of 'technology'. The revelation of it all is so astonishing that Terence McKenna said if you could die by astonishment, you would die by smoking DMT! There is often an intensity in these experiences nothing has prepared us for, and it may take weeks or even years to completely comprehend and recover from a very potent DMT experience. It is no wonder that so many people have so much fear and apprehension about smoking DMT.

We are reminded of the Latin term 'mysterium tremendum', which translates in English as 'overwhelming mystery'. This is the mystery that overwhelms us to the point of fear and trembling; it is one of awe and awe-full-ness, terror and quaking. This is not dissimilar to the fear demanded by the Old Testament god, with its certain sense of immense and imminent wrath and power. This mysterium tremendum is the same state that Muhammad is reported to have experienced when he received the text of the Koran.

As the English novelist Aldous Huxley says in his book about psychedelics, *The Doors of Perception*:

> "The literature of religious experience abounds in references to the pains and terrors overwhelming those who have come, too suddenly, face to face with some manifestation of the mysterium tremendum. In theological language, this fear is due to the incompatibility between man's egotism and the divine purity, between man's self-aggravated separateness and the infinity of God."

There is love within this power, yet this love is not necessarily similar to the romantic love of spring lovers guiding boats through canals as blossoms fall in the water and champagne glasses chime. This loves arises from the very heart of meaning itself – the pulsing electrical charge of the centre of a quantum nuclear power station!

There is something very matter-of-fact about what can be experienced in the DMT state, although the human mind will seemingly never grasp it. So what to do having experienced this? In a sense, after a time, one becomes again an ignorant monkey, often more concerned about bananas and Italian designer luggage, than trying to make sense of these apparently higher realities. To make matters trickier, in Western culture we are typically very serious about many 'things'. Often these beings do not display the same seriousness we do. Or, they display an extremely earnest seriousness, but counter-pointed with an extreme sense of humour and lightness of touch. The theme of many DMT experiences can either be extremely serious and intense, or extremely lighthearted and humorous, or both at the same time. DMT does not normally go halfway. As Ken Wilber has often communicated, paradox is how spirit expresses itself.

Terence McKenna says about DMT:

> "The archetype of DMT is the three-ring circus. The circus is all bright lights, ladies in spangled costumes and wild animals. But right underneath, it's some fairly dark expression of Eros and freaks and unrootedness and mystery. DMT is the quintessence of that archetype. The drug is trying to tell us the true nature of the game. Reality is a theatrical illusion. So you want to find your way to the impresario who produces this and then discuss his next picture with him."

So where do all these visions come from? Early explorers with LSD, the first psychedelic seriously studied in the West, considered the visions to arise from the brain itself, perhaps representing an artifact of consciousness interacting with a drug. The DMT experience, however, seems to be a 'generated' experience rather than resulting from the action of a drug. DMT does not have the action of a drug because it is a neurotransmitter. For most people, the experience of smoking DMT is not something that can simply be continued until one achieves a magical result. For the most part, in any given session, there is a limit to how much magic one will receive. Or, as I like to say, there is only so much 'juice in the jube'. Again, the question of where this magic comes from doesn't make too much sense, as the magic itself is often largely incomprehensible.

For best results, smoked DMT sessions should normally be spaced over a decent time period: at least a week, perhaps even two weeks and more like a month. In that case, the experience can be savoured and the best results will be obtained. There are some people who have smoked DMT or changa every day for a year or even a few years, and found much healing and benefit, yet infrequent smoking is likely to result in much more profound states of being. The decreasing returns you will likely get from the experience may not necessarily be pure 'tolerance', but something perhaps a bit more mysterious and complex. Some people can quite happily smoke DMT all night and keep having good experiences, yet most will hit the wall after some time, and their experiences will start to become darker or repetitive or just not as pleasant. Certainly, the magic will cease to be as present. Seemingly inbuilt to DMT are certain kinds of warning systems. The first few times an individual smokes DMT may well be amazing and magically seductive. Then the rabbit hole starts to appear much deeper and wider than previously anticipated. For so-called 'recreational' users, some more serious experiences may be enough for them to considerably cut back their smoking of DMT, even until they cease to smoke it permanently. In fact, the DMT will often tell people to stop smoking or at least not to smoke DMT casually or recreationally.

This bodes the question, should we even continue to go there at all? My understanding is this. Smoked DMT, high dose changa or even DMT taken by intravenous (IV) or intramuscular (IM) injection is a valuable and extremely powerful experience for human beings to have, although not every human being is ready for this experience. People often say that when you are ready, DMT will come to you – or said in another way: 'when the student is ready, the teacher appears'. Each individual must find their own way with this compound and it seems that each person has their own journey with it, which they must discover. The revelation of changa is that people can smoke DMT for more sub-breakthrough experiences. Even a little bit of DMT, especially combined with herbs like ayahuasca, can connect individuals to a space of personal healing and an inspirational encounter with the sacred. Smoked every so often, every month, every six months or every year, individuals can connect to this consciousness without being blasted into hyperspace, and so this workspace can be incredibly useful and beneficial.

I certainly do not think that DMT is some sort of answer for humanity, as Terence McKenna thought. DMT can reveal an 'a priori' reality, that should lift our spirits and inspire us to live our lives. But I do not believe that suddenly the present domain of human life should somehow be transported to hyperspace or that we must turn our attention to other realms of being as more important than this one. In a sense (as silly as this sounds when written plainly), this has been the religious tendency of man. While we are alive, let us live our lives and not pooh-pooh this world as being lesser or inferior to other worlds. This world communicates to us a use and purpose, so let's live it usefully and purposefully. That has been the very simple message I have always received.

Smoked DMT can be very useful, despite how overwhelmingly powerful and potentially extremely crazy it can be. DMT from plants orally ingested with an monoamine oxidise inhibitor (MAOI) in the form of the ayahuasca vine is normally considered to be more humanly useful than smoked DMT. The smoked DMT experience is so short and overwhelming that most agree it is often quite hard to take very much from it. Changa can allow a longer DMT experience of up to 30 - 60 minutes, especially when successive amounts are smoked, due to the MAOIs in the ayahuasca vine or infused into the herbs, but even this amount of time is often not enough to carry out the necessary inner work. It is in the many hours of an ayahuasca session that one can explore more deeply, and the data that comes through is typically more relevant to one's present lifetime. With ayahuasca or any form of DMT taken orally with an MAO inhibitor, otherworldly journeying is possible, but this is not the primary focus for most people – personal and planetary healing is. When we realise the potentials of our most essential human functionality, we then realise the imperative of fulfilling that functionality to the degree that we can.

Chapter Two

The Meaning of DMT
in the Trees

There is a Neurotransmitter in Acacia Trees

The most that science can say about an acacia tree regarding the alkaloids they can contain, is that a certain percentage of different alkaloids (such as DMT) has been extracted from the tree bark, phyllodes, or root bark. Typical phytochemical analysis of trees (and plants) is normally based upon one alkaloid test from one botanical collection at one time. Such a test clearly cannot tell us the range of alkaloids found in different trees and the differing amounts of those alkaloids, which changes depending on the time of year and also the time of day.

Most phytochemical assays report quite a stable percentage of alkaloids as if this was a consistent factor. For example, it has been commonly stated that *Mimosa hostilis* root bark contains 0.57% DMT (Friedman 1957). However, this is not quite correct as that percentage of DMT was obtained from testing only one particular specimen of *Mimosa hostilis* at one time. Underground researchers report that *Mimosa hostilis* root bark commonly contains between 0.5% to 1% DMT, and with a high yielding batch of inner root bark, 1.5% and even up to 3% DMT is not unheard of. It is also well known that plants will contain different amounts of alkaloids at different times of the year and even over the space of a day. Studies have been carried out on a plantation of *Psychotria viridis* plants which show that the amount of DMT alkaloids is higher at certain times of the day: from as high as 9.52mg/gram (about 0.95% DMT) before dusk, to a smaller amount – 8.97mg/gram at dawn, and almost half as much at midnight – 5.57mg/gram. (J.C. Callaway, 1998)

DMT in Australia is most consistently found in acacia trees growing among granite rocks. In fact, around significant sites of acacia stands, one will almost always find veins of quartz. It may well be that this quartz is somehow useful to the tree in transmitting information, as crystals can be information transmitters – the most simple example being that of the silicon computer chip. In sacred sites of Indigenous Australian significance, one will often find acacia tree species containing DMT. I have seen *Acacia obtusifolia* trees right on the edge of rock formations considered very sacred to indigenous people, and yet nowhere else in the area will these trees be found. *Acacia obtusifolia* trees can be commonly found growing around waterfalls, yet nowhere else in the immediate vicinity. There are also two species of acacia that only grow on one specific mountain, normally on the north facing side of the mountain and only among crystalline granite rocks.

So we must ask, why do these acacia trees contain DMT? Some will say that DMT acts as an insect repellent, but we must take into account that the vast majority of acacia trees do not require DMT in order to successfully repel insects or animals. Even those trees that are known to consistently contain some DMT, such as *Acacia longifolia* or *Acacia obtusifolia*, can also contain cyanogenic glycosides that repel most insects. For an acacia tree to produce an alkaloid such as DMT requires quite a lot of metabolic expenditure – therefore it simply does not make any sense for the tree to produce DMT as an insect repellent, especially in very high amounts. Interestingly, it is often the case that the acacia species in Australia with the highest concentrations of DMT are micro-endemic (i.e. they only grow in one small area). What is even more interesting is that DMT alkaloids extracted from acacias will induce what can only be termed a mystical experience when smoked by human beings. Are we aware of any other kinds of insect repellents in nature that induce visionary experiences in humans?

The Wattle trees that contain DMT command attention with their striking nature. Their phyllodes (strictly defined as stalk-like flattened leaves) are often much larger than that of other acacias. Young *obtusifolia* phyllodes can be almost up to a foot long and their phyllodes are spaced apart from one another in a striking and spiky fashion. If you hold these phyllodes up to the sun, you will see a network of nerves and veins – the most basic signature that indicates an acacia contains DMT. As far as I know, there is no acacia that does not have this signature that contains DMT, yet less than 10% of all acacias possess the feature of anastomisation in the veins of their phyllodes.

The word 'anastomisation' is derived from the Greek word, ἀναστόμωσις (anastomosis), translated as 'communicating opening' or 'to furnish with a mouth or outlet'. The Oxford dictionary defines 'anastomosis' as 'the cross connection between adjacent channels, tubes, fibres, or other parts of a network'. Anastomisation represents a holistic communication within the network of an organism. On the physical level of a phyllode, there is a communication of dissolved ions, hormones and nucleotides within the phyllode. However, not all wattle trees with anastomising veins promise DMT, or even any alkaloid in the acacia. Yet all wattles with phyllodes that contain DMT have anastomising veins in their phyllodes. The only exceptions are the bipinnate acacia species, with their much smaller, feather like leaves – most notably *Mimosa hostilis*, a tree from South America, and some of the Middle Eastern and African acacias. When very young Australian phyllode-bearing acacia seedlings sprout, they begin to grow as bipinnate seedlings. Then they develop phyllodes, which indicates that the development of a phyllode is a newer evolutionary development than bipinnate leaves.

Underground mycelial networks also anastomise, and this type of mycelium gives rise to many mushrooms varieties including mushrooms containing psilocybin (O-phosphoryl-4-hydroxy-N,N-dimethyltryptamine). Anastomisation represents not just the merger of two different streams, but also the interconnectedness of many streams. Streams of water are also known to anastomise, as do quartz crystal veins. Additionally, networks of neurons also anastomise, revealing the brain to be an interconnected processing unit. In the field of botany, it is said that the 'nerves' anastomise within the phyllode or leaf. The definition of a nerve is a fibre or bundle of fibres that transmits impulses. Nerves also imply aliveness and sensation. So what is being transmitted along these nerves? And what could be the meaning of these transmissions?

The Sentience of Plants

Typical scientific human understanding at this time contends that sentience is dependent upon a nervous system and brain. Yet, plants are living tissue. Their internal, spiritual nature is based within their flesh, just as the nature of our life force is indeed not 'within' the nervous system or brain, but an inherent and integrated part of our fleshy makeup. The present day scientific paradigm tends to posit natural life processes in mechanistic terms and typically discounts animistic views that plants have a soul or could, in fact, be aware in a similar way that we are aware, and therefore, possess a kind of sentient intelligence.

If acacia trees are not simply producing DMT for their survival or for their protection from insects, then what are they producing DMT for? It is remarkable that DMT (N,N-dimethyltryptamine) is very similar to one of the primary neurotransmitters in the human brain, serotonin (5-hydroxytryptamine). Simply put, a neurotransmitter allows the transmission of information between neurons. So is it then plausible that the presence of a neurotransmitter in a tree gives us some evidence that the tree possesses one of the primary physical mechanisms of sentience that we possess? My understanding is the trees create a kind of metaphysical field of intelligence through these neurotransmitters via the evident nervous system of veins and nerves in their phyllodes, which appear to receive, transmit and even process information. But what kind of information would the trees be processing, or even communicating?

I cannot adequately answer this question, but what I can say is these trees appear to have a function and a purpose that we would understand as metaphysical, involving the transmission and reception of frequencies to and from realms related to earth and also beyond earth. So if we can come to understand that the trees are transmitting and receiving some sort of information or frequency, what does this communicate to us about human meaning and function? Also, if we humans do not understand our own true meaning and function, then how can we hope to understand the meaning or function of trees?

It is commonly presumed within the Western world that we humans don't have a function or meaning and so just happened to come into existence accidentally. If this is to be believed, then this puts trees in the same category as us. They just randomly happen to exist, and because their existence is just an accident, there is no meaning or function they can have beyond survival. If they happen to contain potent neurotransmitters, then that is also an accident, and does not have to have any reason or significance. These kinds of views are indicative of the dead-end nihilism of materialism, which could be perceived as a quaint and somewhat primitive stage in humanity's development.

Scientific materialist reductionism will communicate only what is most evident and physically measurable through the present system of interpretation. As it stands, if we stay with what we can currently measure (or try to measure) in the realm of the physical domain, we will not come up with anything significant or meaningful, but rather only static data that gives priority to external values, which remain largely consistent, mechanical, and meaningless. From this viewpoint, we must give little credibility to internal values that shift and move like waves – like emotions. But in fact, emotions, thoughts and other largely non-measurable phenomena are our primary and most immediate reality as human beings. And what are emotions and thoughts but a kind of frequency?

So why would this frequency be occurring? And why would we be occurring or why are we occurring? I perceive that our function, in terms of the natural world, is to radiate or transmit a frequency that is felt by us internally and is, perhaps, measurable. The transmission and reception of this frequency gives us a feeling of well-being and satisfaction and accords to 'happiness'. The frequency of being most esteemed by humans is what we call 'love' in the English language. My perspective is that love is the recognition of frequency, the generation of frequency, the approval of frequency! That frequency is unique and individual – it is a radiance, an expression of beingness. When we feel it, we know what it is. It seems to me that the trees are radiating a kind of frequency of aliveness and they have their own inner world, as we humans have our own inner world. Then it stands to reason that the trees have a particular meaning and fruition in their aliveness, as each human being has a felt sense of aliveness and meaning in themselves.

Australian Acacia Species Containing DMT

Most of the well-known Australian acacia species containing DMT are categorised in the 'juliflora' section with anastomising veins. Some of these trees are rare, growing on only one mountain or area. However, on the east coast of Australia, species such as *Acacia obtusifolia* and *Acacia floribunda* can often be very viable sources of tryptamines. On the west coast, the relatively common *Acacia acuminata* is a very good source of tryptamines. DMT is found in the phyllodes of all *Acacia acuminata* strains, from around 0.1 - 0.5% in winter and going up to around 1.5% in the springtime, but generally being around 0.5 - 0.6 %, and also showing a lot of variance in the many different strains of this species.

The phyllodes of some of the *Acacia floribunda* strains with fine anastomisation contain around 0.2 - 0.4% DMT, although some of the strains with less anastomisation may contain 0.1% to almost no DMT. *Acacia floribunda* bark from the right strains, generally contains from 0.3% - 0.5% DMT.

The picking of phyllodes from these trees is clearly the most sustainable way of wild harvesting tryptamines for human usage. *Acacia obtusifolia* phyllodes may often not be useable, because the alkaloids that are extracted may not contain a high enough percentage of DMT compared to the bark, with the resulting extracts often being more oily and gummy rather than crystalline, containing a high proportion of mysterious alkaloids compared to DMT. The amount of DMT obtainable from the *obtusifolia* phyllodes is typically very low to nonexistent in many strains – such as those found in the Blue Mountains or north of Sydney. Also, there are likely to be cyanide-like compounds in *Acacia obtusifolia* phyllodes, as there are known to be in *Acacia longifolia* phyllodes and bark as well, which makes them unsuitable for brews. However, I have tested phyllodes from *Acacia obtusifolia* strains a few hours south of Sydney and found them to contain 0.5% crystalline DMT. The phyllodes tasted 'grassy' and so it is likely that such strains could be used in ayahuasca brews. One reliable researcher has communicated to me that in most strains of *obtusifolia* on the south coast of NSW, the phyllodes and twigs contain around 0.3 - 0.7% of very useable DMT, but may also contain varying amounts of the largely inactive N-Methyltryptamine (NMT).

Acacia obtusifolia bark contains from 0.1 to 0.9% DMT, but normally containing around 0.3 - 0.5% DMT. *Acacia obtusifolia* bark may also be used to make a tea taken with Syriun Rue (*Peganum harmala)* or Ayahuasca vine (*Banisteriopsis caapi)* to make it orally active, but it can contain a lot of tannins, making it difficult to drink. *Acacia obtusifolia* bark can also contain a lot of other alkaloids apart from DMT, including 5-MeO-DMT, Bufotenine and maybe up to as many as a few dozen different alkaloids, which have not been well studied. I once discovered a stand of *obtusifolias*, containing an alkaloid in the phyllodes, which would catalyse a 6 hour journey not dissimilar to mushrooms, when only 10mg of the extract was smoked!

Common strains of *Acacia longifolia* have generally been found to be low yielding in the bark and phyllodes (around 0.1 - 0.2% DMT), although there have been some successful reports of very useable extractions from this species. *Acacia maidenii* is the acacia tree most commonly mentioned by those who have done some limited Internet research into the wattles, although out of the many reports from individuals I have met, most say the yield they obtain from this tree is in the area of 0.1 - 0.2%, or nothing at all. It also seems that there are many different strains of this tree. One acquaintance says he has obtained 0.5% DMT from the phyllodes of *Acacia maidenii*, from a certain small stand of trees around Sydney. Other reports of worthwhile extractions from this tree are quite hard to come by. What is quite interesting to note is that the anastomisation present in both of these typically low yielding trees, *Acacia maidenii* and *Acacia longifolia*, is highly unimpressive. You can often barely see connectiveness between the veins (just the occasional bridge between longitudinal nerves), whereas the higher yielding species almost always have a pattern of very intricate cross-connecting veins in the phyllodes.

Acacia courtii and *Acacia phlebophylla* deserve a mention because they each only grow on one mountain, which means they are micro-endemic. Some people are very protective of these trees and say that human beings should stay well away from them. But I would say each tree has a different kind of wisdom, a different message, a different teaching. We should endeavour to grow these trees away from their mountain homes so that future generations can benefit from their unique teachings. Fortunately, some researchers are taking up this challenge.

Acacia phlebophylla only grows on Mount Buffallo, in North East Victoria, and was first reported to contain DMT, in the Australian Journal of Chemistry article in 1967. Contrary to this initial phytochemical testing, *phlebophylla* phyllodes do not consistently contain 0.3% DMT, but more commonly 0.4-0.6% DMT and even up 1% DMT.

Acacia courtii primarily grows on one small mountain near the sea, on the north coast of New South Wales – and even then, only on the north facing aspect of the mountain in steep areas of granite rock, just above the suburban houses of a small town. Underground researchers have determined that the bark from this species generally contains around 0.4 - 1% DMT and the phyllodes contain around 1 - 1.2% DMT. What is very interesting about this tree is that its branches often hang right down to the ground like willow trees, as if they were designed to be picked. I have not noticed such low hanging branches in any other species of acacia. Even with very large *Acacia courtii* trees, there are always branches hanging down that can easily be taken without affecting the growth of the tree. In fact, there often seems to be too much growth. It could be perceived that taking some branches tidies up the way the tree is growing and prevents the tree from being pulled down by the weight of its branches and phyllodes on their steep mountain home. However, do remember that most of these trees lie within national parks and taking plant matter, even if it is phyllodes, is illegal. In Australia, people have been seriously prosecuted for taking plant matter from national parks, as it is considered a very serious offence. Also, fungus has been noticed growing on *Acacia courtii* populations, likely caused by people pruning branches using unclean secateurs.

I have found tryptamines in the Australian bipinnate wattle *Acacia mearnsii*, although identification is very tricky, as I have found in depth botanical classification carried out on the acacia genus in Australia is very much incomplete. I would say there is very little consistency as to when trypt-amines are present in the Australian bipinnate species. I get the impres-sion the same issue exists with the African and Middle Eastern bipinnate acacia species, based upon my limited firsthand research on acacia trees in these regions.

There are many other acacia trees containing DMT, of course. This is a young field where explorers often do not share notes with each other, and so much research has yet to be carried out. However, DMT has been found in dozens of different tree species all over Australia, yet the yields are often relatively quite low (around 0.1 - 0.3%), which may make brewing and ex-tracting from these trees not as worthwhile as from higher yielding trees. However, much research is yet to be done and modern day researchers have only scratched the surface into understanding this mysterious genus of tree and why and when it secretes DMT.

The Harvesting of Acacias

Most acacias have a limited life span from 30 to 60 years and then after this time, they will often start to die and then fall over. If the trees are growing on a mountains, they will often simply fall over due to changing environ-mental conditions, thunderstorms, and loose soil. DMT extractors will sometimes cut down a whole acacia tree for its bark, although some may exaggerate the effect of their harvesting. Harvesters will generally choose the older trees that are on their way out within months or years. These are also often the largest trees and are perceived to contain the most wisdom and power. A conscious harvester will make contact with the land and in-tuitively know where to walk to find trees and will also know the right tree to harvest. Many people will communicate and ask the tree for permission to proceed with the harvesting. Often it is the case that the trees which give that permission are on their way to falling over, and are starting to rot on the outside and inside. Many harvesters will just wait for a storm to come through and only take the trees that have been knocked down. However, not all harvesters are particularly conscious, and some are unaware they are dealing with sentient beings.

In some state forests, where DMT-containing acacia trees are growing, one will often find commercial loggers indiscriminately cutting down huge areas of trees. Acacia harvesters would likely take in a year as many trees as loggers cut down in a day. Put into that context, small scale harvesting of acacia trees for their DMT does not really seem worth getting too upset about. Also, many people fail to see that most of these acacia trees in Australia are inaccessible to human beings, in deep bushland, far away from any roads or tracks. Of course, it is important to be aware of and respect the trees as living beings and to make sure that the right trees are taken. This means that the tree itself gives permission to be harvested, which is a fundamental factor in the resulting DMT being friendly and truly usable by human beings. All this is written with the understanding that these actions are going to be carried out by individuals and groups, whether other individuals or groups agree or not.

It appears to me that the trees are inherently complicit in this activity of harvesting and resulting consumption. After all, we humans are hunter-gatherers, and it is generally the case that the DMT is going to be used by the tribe, for the advancement of the tribe. This needs to be made clear to the trees. The trees probably take themselves a lot more seriously than we humans do, and also a lot less seriously – which is perhaps their paradox. Those who indiscriminately harvest trees without having an awareness they are dealing with living beings, often find themselves facing great troubles and stresses in their lives, and this is a commonly observed phenomenon. As the saying goes, powerful plants have powerful allies. What is of most concern however, is not people who cut down a tree or two, but those who cut down or ring bark multiple trees, even a few dozen trees. Indiscriminate, unconscious, large scale harvesting of this nature is a real threat to many wild populations of Acacias, damages our relationship with the species and results in an inferior quality of DMT.

In the coming decades, we must make sure to grow these trees ourselves, so that human beings are not reliant on wild harvesting for the tryptamines that are so valuable as agents of awakening human awareness. And again it is worth saying, that there are so many acacia trees that fall over in the bush, that there is already an abundance of DMT available in the wild, so cutting down acacia trees is not often necessary. It is also worth noting that those who take strips of bark from acacias will very often kill the tree, as the trees are then exposed to borers and other predators.

Those living in Western Australia are lucky enough to be able to pick the phyllodes of high yielding *Acacia Acuminata* trees, which generally contain from 0.5 to 1.5% DMT. Clearly, *Acacia Acuminata* is the highest DMT yielding acacia which can be most easily grown by people in different parts of the world, and it is also the acacia that is most easily harvested in a sustainable manner.

Drinking an Acacia Floribunda Brew

Acacia floribunda is a tree that grows quite commonly up and down the Australian eastern seaboard. I was somewhat reticent to try a brew made from its phyllodes because it often does not show particularly detailed anastomising in its veins, and also does not display the same thick, stiff phyllodes of the other acacias containing DMT.

A friend pruned a large number of branches from a 30-foot high *Acacia floribunda* growing in his yard, so I took some of the branches from his lawn, and when I got home, plucked some of the dried phyllodes from the branches and cooked up 200 grams. I added water over the top of the phyllodes and less than a cup of apple cider vinegar and simmered it for a couple of hours. Then I reduced the brew very slowly, down to 650ml.

I have noticed acacia brews tend to get destroyed if they are brewed down too far, and it is likely that excessive heat that destroys the DMT. But if you boil the brew down really slowly, at a very low heat, then the brew will likely remain unaffected.

I took the brew to a group I was facilitating – just a small group of five people in a beautiful house in the Dandenongs, just outside of Melbourne. First we drank four grams of a very good batch of Syrian rue seeds in a brew of 40 mls of liquid. Everyone reported the rue to be happy, bright and opening – even though four grams is a strong dose, and three grams will normally suffice to effect MAO inhibition, which allows the DMT to not be broken down by the MAO enzymes.

I poured a cup of what must have be less than 200mls, thinking maybe I would drink half of that, which would be equivalent to 35 grams or so of phyllodes. I took three very small sips of the *floribunda* brew, and immediately it hit me like an enveloping electric unfurling. So then I lay down and let it work on me. In my visual field, I saw acacia-like branches and then felt it working on my energy body, twisting, turning, and coming up through my core. Never before had such a small amount affected me in the same way. I was happy to let this go on for some time, thinking maybe I should drink some more and at least get a good taste for this plant. So I drank half the glass in a few glugs. Its taste was bitter, but not too bad, and there was something earthier about it than most acacia brews, which can be quite astringent.

Soon there were more visions, and I had a really good sense of the tree. It felt very benevolent and kind; down to earth. It showed me a picture of an Australian aboriginal person, not like we see them, but more like they actually were. It was a very good portrait with many fine features, like a photograph. Then to the left of that, a cartoon image of an aboriginal person, showing me how the tree perceived how white people saw aboriginal people – simply as a caricature, not as real people.

There were many communications like this that I couldn't quite decipher at times, just receive and view. The imagery was not overtly colourful, but it was deep and had the quality of black and white art photography – of a sort of silvery look with depth and dimensions. I had entered the world of the tree not quite fully, but fully enough. The plant opened up channels in my body I had never felt touched by any other plant. The effect was more like 5-MeO-DMT than DMT, and I could not discount the presence of that compound. There was a force to it that was so gentle and yet penetrating. I could not say there was anything going on with my 'chakras', more like the tree was pushing up through a central tube of energy along my spine. At times there was slight pain, but it was an exquisite sensation where there had been numbness. It was awakening pain not 'there is something wrong here' pain; the difference is quite clear, as often there is pleasure after this pain, the feeling that something has released.

Immediately, I felt very comfortable with this tree. Most of the other acacias containing DMT have a special, rare or exclusive quality about them. This tree was very 'down to earth'. It reminds me of when I extracted alkaloids from a bipinnate tree I was able to identify as the quite common *Acacia mearnsii* in northeast Victoria. I did dozens of tests on *Acacia mearnsii* and only found 1.1% DMT in this one tree in April. I even went back to the same tree at another time and didn't find any alkaloids in it. The experience of smoking the extract was of such benevolence and friendliness, with the tree giving me the feeling of the sun smiling on earth.

Who knows how many human beings had ever communed with *floribunda* in an oral brew before this time? Certainly not very many Caucasians at least. For sure, there was a certain purity to the experience, missing in the DMT from acacia species humans typically extract and utilise. I did not know of anyone taking *Acacia floribunda* in this way before this time, so there is perhaps an element of the tree wanting to make a good impression. In fact, I'm pretty certain of it. In the days after the experience, I felt opened up and clearer, less fallible, and glad to have experienced a new plant ally.

Chapter Three

Espiritu Naturale

How the Plants can Work with Us

Many psychoactive plants typically communicate very directly with the individual who chooses to ingest their flesh. A lot of people will feel comfortable letting these plants know their deepest secrets, in addition to their present thoughts and feelings. For many of us, this sort of openness is quite different to how we operate in the world, obscuring the actuality of what we are thinking and feeling. In the corporeal world we may fear being judged as we often do judge. It is not that the plants do not judge (as they have their own assessments of reality that could appear to us to be a form of judgment). But it is often very easy to feel comfortable with them, in part because they do not exist within our immediate circle of influence. There is a feeling of intimacy that one can have with them – you can feel safe in a way that you may not often feel with human beings.

A common perspective of the traditional, archetypal shaman or priest, is that as the healer of the village, he (or she) is supposed to remain out of its worldly affairs. He often does not accept any money, practices celibacy, and does not engage in worldly activities. You come to him for confession because he can offer you counsel. You can trust him and share deeply personal material, because he has no investment in worldly life. You know you will not have to deal with him on a personal level, in your worldly affairs, or consider the possibility that he is competing with you in business or could have an affair with your wife. The plant is similar in this regard, but the plant is totally out of the human world altogether, and in this 'confession', the plant is not going to disclose what it sees and hears to other human beings.

However, as apparently thorough as these plants appear to be in the psychological, therapeutic, and energetic healing work they carry out, they cannot 'get to' everything that is troubling us as human beings. Neither can we necessarily, in our human-to-human 'psychotherapeutic' framework, work out all of what is troubling to us through 'talking therapy'. There are certain layers and levels in the human being, which the plants can be especially effective at treating. But there may be structural issues on the musculo-skeletal level that only skilled and able osteopaths, chiropractors or bodyworkers can address. Additionally, there are other levels of human consciousness which can be accessed through the meridians or bio-energetic system, which talented acupuncturists or spiritual healers can effectively address. I have also found vibrational remedies, such as gem essences or flower essences, can affect profound healing and realignment that no human being or regular plant medicine can easily reach.

Moreover, it is my view that every person living in the West would do well to look into detoxification via colonics and/or juice fasting and taking psyllium husks with bentonite clay. These basic processes remove mucoid plaque and various wastes that inhibit the effective and healthy functioning of the body, as the body alone cannot easily deal with the typically complex and often toxic Western style of diet and the enormous amounts of synthetic chemicals prevalent in the modern day environment. I have also found colonic irrigation to be just as powerful as ayahuasca (even more so at times) when it comes to healing the psycho-dynamics of my physical and energetic body. For example, I have found colonics have repeatedly released chronic tension in my neck that no other treatment has ever affected. Many have found ayahuasca detoxifying and cleansing, but I think ayahuasca is no substitute for an intelligent diet and persistent detoxification. This might sound like a minor matter to some, but so much of the typical Western diet can be problematic to being in a state of good health, and this is no news to those who have inquired into this issue.

Common Western mental orientations and perspectives are often not inclined to address present human issues and tend to presume that the present psychosocial paradigm is in a state of balance. As such, many Western psycho-spiritual practices and processes appear like cross-training for the mind, body and soul, and may not consider any particular collective imbalance, unevolved or confused cultural patterns or variously complex causes of mental, psychic, or emotional ill health. This tendency is, of course, the human egoic inclination, but it is obviously the case that there are many problematic issues we humans face, collectively and culturally. Furthermore, there are many attitudes and approaches within different cultures which can take time to understand. The good news is that with an open mind and a sensitive awareness, we can become mindful of what is at hand that is causing suffering, preventing evolution and fruitful mental, emotional and spiritual functionality.

Western psychiatric models value the 'normal' standard, which is clearly a self-important fallacy, especially when it is clear that what is normal in one culture is completely abnormal in another. One of the things the plants can show us is how far as humans we have to go to truly reach our potential. The plants tend to make us aware of our shortcomings and can also give us a direct experience of our potential. The plants have always reiterated to me that we in the West are profoundly disconnected from ourselves, the natural world, and our own powers. The global human enterprise of capitalism regards numbers on a screen to have significantly more value than the humans who created the numbers on the screen, or the ecosystem that allowed those numbers to exist on the screen in the first place. This is of course, a completely disconnected and insane view of reality. The plants have no qualms about showing us our insanity; and if we are open to listening, they can help us see how we can become sane, connected to nature, each other, and the aeon. But first, we must become aware of that disconnection and truly realise the information inherent within our own suffering before we can become connected and integrated with what is at hand. Then, at the very least, we can begin to understand the possibilities of our inter-connected intelligence, essential functionality, and a much vaster definition of true health than simply physical or mental functionality.

Mescaline from the Cactus

Mescaline-containing cactus is a true medicine for the mind and body, and a medicine for many other aspects of our nature that many may not recognise. Mescaline has a certain reputation in popular culture as a very strong and psychedelic visual agent, which is not entirely accurate. Most people are more aware of mescaline-containing peyote (*Lophophora williamsii*) than mescaline-containing San Pedro (*Echinopsis pachanoi*) or dozens of other mescaline-containing cacti. The issue here is that peyote only grows in certain areas of North America and is known to be endangered in the wild. Even if you do manage to obtain some fresh peyote from the wild, a miraculous vision quest experience is not guaranteed, unless an extremely concentrated brew is made from the buttons, as eating the raw buttons is very hard work due to their very strong taste. Peyote is primarily a pure agent of immense spiritual healing and like all the mescaline-containing cacti, the spirit of peyote presents itself to carry out healing work, not necessarily to entertain you or show you visions.

San Pedro cactus is much more common than peyote and is prevalent throughout Mexico and South America. Mescaline is the primary alkaloid in both succulents, so the effects of San Pedro are very similar to peyote. The mescaline-containing cacti tend not to be prepared to entertain humans with visual elements like many other plants. In fact, one way to see it is that most plants are not prepared to communicate with human beings through their visionary capacity. And by far the most visual psychoactive is not a plant, but a fungus – psilocybin-containing magic mushrooms. None of the mescaline-containing cacti are known to be particularly proactive plant teachers. They seem to prefer to work on interior aspects of the human organism, rather than directly communicate with the human mind. Although powerful visionary communications are possible from taking cactus, especially with the much stronger doses that many are reluctant to ingest.

Mescaline-containing cactus especially focuses upon carrying out work on the somatic levels of being. After ingesting the dried or fresh flesh or a tea made from up to a foot of the green outer flesh, people will often experience a clarity of internal and outer awareness. Terence McKenna discounted mescaline as a serious material for exploration because he considered it a type of amphetamine and concluded that amphetamines are bad for the health, therefore mescaline must be too. However, most amphetamines stimulate the central nervous system, while mescaline primarily stimulates the peripheral nervous system. It appears to me that the cactus is working on this system of the body's nerves and 'ganglia' from the inside. I know of one man who took cactus and experienced a healing that enabled him to dance, after many years of physically not being able to due to injury. Perhaps for many, cactus will be less of a material for exploration and more of a quintessential plant teacher and healer. Even among those who take enough cacti (which is quite hard to do, often even for those who understand how best to prepare it) very few seem truly inspired to go deeply into what it can teach.

One of the best ways I have found of taking cactus is to take it with a group of people walking in nature, even a group of up to 20 or 30 people at a time. The cactus experience is very conducive to movement, whereas if you take cactus in a sitting group or circle, its effects are not always so potent that sitting still for six to ten hours is an ideal situation. 'Cactus walks' are great fun, easy to organise and include elements of getting out in nature, exercising, meeting new people, sharing food, medicine, laughter and good conversation.

People generally feel clearer, healthier and more invigorated after taking mescaline-containing cactus. In my own case, I can feel the cactus working on me, particularly in clearing blockages in my liver, which makes sense, as the function of the liver is directly related to the function of the peripheral nervous system. Of course, Western medical science views the liver's function on a purely physical level. Only in ancient systems, such as Chinese medicine, does the liver have a metaphysical meaning, and in that system the liver organ and its corresponding meridian line is strongly related to the emotions.

In the first lines of Dostoyevsky's *Notes from The Underground*, the protagonist says:

> "I am a sick man... I am a spiteful man. I am an unattractive man. I believe my liver is diseased. However, I know nothing at all about my disease and do not know for certain what ails me."

He then goes on to say that he has never seen a doctor for what he believes ails him – and what ails him is clearly a psychological condition that he experiences as being centred in his liver. The protagonist has clearly connected the condition of his psyche with the condition of his body. What would any doctor say to someone who said they were sick and spiteful and that their liver was diseased? I doubt many Western doctors would be able to diagnose the disease of this character. Most likely the doctor would shoo him away and tell him there is nothing wrong with his liver (on a functional level). But the point is, he feels there is something wrong with his liver. It is likely a Chinese herbalist would prescribe some herbs to treat imbalances and blockages in his liver. When I take good Chinese herbal medicine for my liver, it definitely feels like there is a moving and shifting of energy or 'chi'.

So if this character took ten good doses of cactus over ten weeks, I would suggest his liver might feel less diseased to him! He also might feel a lot better after taking Chinese medicine. Yet the difference between working with cactus as compared to Chinese herbs (or indeed herbs from any culture to treat imbalances in the liver) is that with cactus you are dealing with the intricate psychic layers of the human mind and psyche, as well the body. In one session with cactus, I could feel and see alphabet letters in my liver as if there was verbal programming becoming unblocked, and then I felt a sense of release and freedom in that part of my body and in my entire being.

What the cactus shows me, at times, is a view of inside the human body, which looks something like scientific videos of ganglia and associated functions of the nervous system. I cannot interpret this information too clearly, but I can see there is something special taking place, and what's more, I can feel it. I doubt it would be easy for present-day science to map exactly what is going on when an individual takes mescaline. What seems most important to realise is that the active intelligence of the cactus is carrying out this work. Again, how that intelligence works is not well understood – but that this work occurs is unmistakable to those experienced with sharing cactus in medicine circles. To most experienced explorers with plants, the reductionist understanding that molecules are simply molecular structures 'agonising' receptor sites is simply not taken seriously. For many people working with cactus intensively, it is on the somatic and emotional aspects of human beings that the cactus is perceived to be primarily working.

Synthetic phenethylamine compounds like 2C-B (based on the mescaline molecule) are human inventions – and so it is that human issues will especially tend to come to the surface with 2C-B. It is then a matter of processing and dealing with these realisations in a way that works for the individual. These processes can be quite intense and 2C-B may have a relatively limited 'recreational' appeal for a lot of people, as what arises in one's awareness can be quite confronting. Once I brought together a small group of people, and we all took around 18mg of 2C-B. We sat in a circle, and in that space, through the theatre of freestyle spoken word and sing-ing, occurred a collective realisation and understanding. Could this type of freestyle group be as effective if the participants took cactus? Of course it could, but there is something empty in 2C-B that allows humans to fill the space with their own psychic and mental material.

However, for sensitive people there is often something very uncomfortable about these synthetic chemical compounds. For many, the discomfort will override any value they may gain from ingesting them. I personally find these synthetic compounds are very harsh and hard on the body. Assuming the continued progression and development of the human race, I doubt people will work with them in a hundred years' time or feel a need to do so. Maybe in a hundred years there will be other synthetic compounds, which 'mesh' and integrate with the body much more easily and help us to unlock its powers. Yet, I suspect we will not need such compounds in order to unlock the human potential.

Changa

I developed and dubbed the DMT smoking blend known as 'changa' (which I pronounce as chang-ah) in 2003-2004. People often ask me how changa came to be, and this is explained in two articles that can be found in the ap-pendix. Changa is a blend of conducive herbs infused with DMT, normally including ayahuasca vine and leaf, which enables DMT to be experienced at more sub-breakthrough levels rather than the breakthrough experiences people generally like to have smoking freebase crystal DMT.

The breakthrough DMT experience is typically so overwhelming that few are keen to go there too often, hence the amount of crystal DMT in any given community is normally quite small. The kind of sub-breakthrough experiences that changa typically enables, while not normally as over-whelming as the breakthrough experiences people typically reach with DMT, are just as valuable and valid. DMT smoked in changa form can be gentle and its benefits can be reaped from semi-regular use, whereas there are not many people who continually reach back for crystal DMT and their pipe for regular breakthrough immersions. Most people seem to have up to a two-year honeymoon period with DMT, after which their usage of it tends to decrease considerably, as at that point, they normally have received the meat of the meaning of the messages that DMT can deliver.

In many places around the world, changa seems to have largely replaced all forms of crystal DMT. Many people have realised that changa lasts longer, is easier to smoke, and the visual experience is often superior; it is also easier to transport and looks less like a nefarious illegal drug than crystal DMT. What's more, the changa experience tends to be very similar to a mini ayahuasca experience. People can benefit from the healing qualities of the ayahuasca vine and have an experience that tends to be more integrated and grounding than smoking freebase DMT crystal.

It is often the case with DMT that more is less, and many Western people with their egoic ambition often forget that. Some people are making 60 to 80% DMT changa blends, forsaking the herbal elements that give so much richness to the experience. Changa that is predominately DMT, with a small concentration of herbs, is far too strong for many people. I have met a number of people who were casually passed a pipe of strong changa and were terrified by what happened to them, as they were not at all prepared for a full-blown DMT experience. Whereas a changa blend of 25 to 35% DMT or so would not normally create such intense and possibly frightening effects. There is no doubt that DMT can be powerful beyond belief and for many, the breakthrough DMT experience is not easily assimilated at all.

The presence of ayahuasca and the other herbs in changa allows the DMT experience to be more integrated with the human biological awareness. Changa was designed to harness that power in a way that can be usefully assimilated by people.

One primary advantage of changa over the ayahuasca brew is its availability and accessibility to more people and the shortness of its duration, compared to ayahuasca brews, which are normally expensive and only available from 'shamans' in typically quasi-traditional ceremonies in the big cities of certain countries, normally costing quite a lot of money. Perhaps the primary disadvantage of changa is the harshness of the smoke, although when changa contains lung herbs like mullein or coltsfoot it should be much easier to smoke than crystal DMT. For this reason, I would encourage people to be very wary of continual, non-occasional use, as the smoke from the DMT seems more harmful to me than smoke from tobacco or cannabis.

The other primary disadvantage of changa (and this could be said of all psychedelics) is that opening up doorways and engaging into these extra-dimensional states of consciousness can really unsettle the human organism in many different ways. It may not be useful to open these doors to other dimensions continually or to keep them open, as the resulting data and connectedness to these realms and beings can become distracting or overly occupying for many aspects of our humanity, which can leave some people ungrounded and unable to focus on their earthly life.

Very early on, I could see how changa would be mixed up with all the different kinds of compounds and drugs that people take, and that some people would simply see changa as another escapist drug. I also saw that it could not be held back from the world stage and that while it would fall into the hands of those who would not truly respect or understand its power and value, it would also fall on respectful and fertile ground, where it would have the most incredible results and naturally inspire people to use it in very respectful and creative circumstances.

It is clear to me that changa is a valid medicine and agent of awakening – and that much of what it exposes, visually and aesthetically, is awesome and inspiring, feeding authentic richness, beauty, and depth into people's awareness. That it is often enjoyable does not mean that the experience is not fruitful or that it is a merely recreational experience. The diversity of what people will experience by smoking changa is immense, although most of the data that people receive is going to be visual, and just as with aya-huasca, a healing and a clearing of the body's circuitry is a strong element of the experience. After a good changa experience you should feel very good, even reborn in some instances. Many internal alignments may occur very quickly, as various systems of the body are given an immediate reference point for being in tune. What individuals are going to gain from that experience is dependent on where they are at and what their intention is. What changa comes down to is an experience which is going to be quite short: normally between 10 and 20 minutes, with after-effects of heightened senses and perhaps a warm glowing feeling lasting for up to an hour or so.

If you are seriously going to smoke changa, it is best to smoke it in a water bong or pipe by yourself or with someone else holding the pipe and helping you to smoke it. You should try to smoke the herbs down in one go if you can, and then hold the smoke in as long as you can (within reason), and then breathe the smoke out through the nose – as this appears to connect the DMT more closely with centres in the brain, like the pineal gland. Another good way to smoke changa is to pass around a changa joint, rolled without any other herbs, sharing it with a circle of people, in order to sit in silence or sing. Like all so-called 'drugs', there's a social element of sharing changa, and it is clear that sharing strong experiences can be bonding between friends and individuals. I have been to a wedding where two changa joints were passed around by the groom: a 30% blend at around 10pm and a 50% blend (to go a few levels deeper!) at 2am – which left the participants in a state of awe, amazement and gratitude.

Psilocybin Mushrooms

Perhaps the most underrated way to consume psilocybin mushrooms is to grind up dried mushrooms and make mushroom chocolate. It is actually very easy to make your own raw chocolate, using a third each of cacao butter, raw cacao power and raw sugar or agave syrup. You will then need to melt the cacao butter, mix the ingredients together and add them to a mould, measuring the amounts of chocolate so that if one mould contains 20 grams, each 20 grams of your chocolate contains 1 dried gram of ground mushroom powder. Taking mushrooms this way is easy, and you don't even taste the mushrooms, the come on is very smooth and the chocolate helps with absorption and slightly potentiates the effects of the mushrooms, because it contains small amounts of MAO inhibitors such as tetrahydro-beta-carbolines.

Taking 1 gram of dried psilocybin every week has helped me to deal with living in the city. There are enormous amounts of toxic elements in modern life: air pollution, chemical pollutants and EMF pollution, and I have found that mushrooms can help to clear these effects. As a tonic, and I take many different tonic herbs and teas all the time, I believe psilocybin mushrooms to be one of the most potent available - just as potent as ayahuasca and sometimes even more effective when taken with this intent of clearing and healing the body. For me 1 dried gram is very much a medicinal dose, and apart from some mental clarity and physical energy, there is not much more to it. Of course, different mushrooms will vary in their strength. Two grams of some mushrooms strains can be quite potent, while I've had 5 grams of home grown *Psilocybe Cubensis* mushrooms that were quite weak and wafty, perhaps due to the nature of the people who grew them and what they wanted from them.

2 - 3 dried grams is a dose in which you can walk around and experience some startling visual effects, but not be too overwhelmed. Over 4 grams to 10 grams is where the more visionary effects occur, which can often be quite similar to a visionary ayahuasca experience or smoking DMT. I've personally found great value in taking a few grams of dried mushrooms, whether alone in a bedroom or with a partner, playing music and being introspective. Of course, this practice goes for all psychedelics. It is really a matter of setting aside time and understanding the value of the revelations and realisation that can occur. I have found taking mushrooms in small groups with people singing and playing instruments is a very good setting of people and circumstance. Although, mushrooms do not typically work too well when taken in bigger social gatherings or at parties.

Terence McKenna famously said that taking 5+ dried grams alone in a dark room was THE way to get the most from the mushroom. Explorers such as Kilindi Iyi propose even higher doses of mushrooms as a valid path, and he suggests 20 to 30 grams as an upper limit. The most I have taken is 9 dried grams, and for me that dose was very intense, very similar to a high dose ayahuasca experience. For most people, I would say the most they would ever want to take is 10 - 15 grams. Sometimes, when I used to take a big plateful of fresh mushrooms, I would blackout and not remember what happened to me. As with all tryptamines, you know you have taken too much when you black out. With all the emphasis on Ayahuasca, high dose mushrooms are as extraordinary and magical as Ayahuasca, if not more so at times, and tend not to be so much focused on facing shadow material, but more inter-dimensional perspectives.

There is so much hype regarding Ayahuasca, people forget that psilocybin mushrooms are natures most available tryptamine. You can find them growing in almost all areas of the world. In Europe, *Psilocybe semilanceata*, which grows in autumn, can be found in northern Scandinavia, right down to mid-Italy. Many explorers with extensive experience with Iboga, Ayahuasca and Cactus prefer psilocybin mushrooms most of all. There are some people, frustrated that the DMT admixture plants normally combined with ayahuasca sometimes don't produce visionary effects, use mushrooms instead with the ayahuasca vine. This combination is very potent and it is a rule of thumb that mushrooms with an MAO inhibitor like Syrian rue or Ayahuasca will double their strength with the MAOI.

For me, the nature of the mushroom experience depends on the strain of the mushroom and where it is grown. I have found 'shit loving' wild *Psilocybin cubensis* mushrooms that grow on cow dung to sometimes produce random and undesirable effects, and I have come to prefer carefully grown homemade *cubensis* mushrooms. Wild wood loving mushrooms, which in Australia grow in the winter, are clearer in my experience and more potent than 'shit loving' mushrooms. While the most potent and magical species of mushrooms I have found grow around the far north coast of NSW in the Nightcap ranges, and that some claim are *Psilocybe subaeruginascens* (Voogelbreinder 2009). However, I know one researcher who claims to have found over half a dozen new species of psilocybin containing mushrooms in that area alone, which may indicate how much there is still to know about psilocybin containing mushrooms.

I believe that each species of psilocybin mushrooms produces an entirely different type of experience. This goes against the views of those who say that a molecule is a molecule, and because there cannot be difference in the psilocybin molecule, any difference in effect must be due to other factors. Yet, experienced explorers well understand the stark differences between different psilocybin containing mushrooms from around the world.

—

Below are two Mushroom experiences from 2001 and 2002 respectively, when I encountered beings who came and performed surgery upon me, something that has happened to me with ayahuasca and DMT as well, and this a commonly experienced theme for those who ingest tryptamines.

—

Sitting down and smoking a rolly cigarette, I close my eyes and a sound and visual field opens up, into a graceful flurorescent amorphous intelligence, rippling red and white like glass - moving towards me, a continuum of being. It ever so gently touches and sweeps around me, pulsing and checking. And with my eyes closed I can see my surroundings as it comes through, opening a curtain down one side and then to another. Ultra clear human hands flash signals of contact and touch, and "Here I am, okay?" One part is of this being is resting on the right of my head and another on my stomach.

Above my stomache, it presented images of a vacuum cleaner, revealing such a slick humour of operation. Around my head, they are checking, taking measurements, balancing with a profound internal technology, as if they are replacing cards and software, codes of some kind, reorganising my brain, very organically, and comfortably.

Then in a minute they withdraw back, with such a graceful flourish, a twirling inherent dance; showing me that their nature translated into human terms is a large handsome New York transsexual woman nurse! Their departure is of such implicit lyricism, continuity and gentleness.

These kind of operations have happened a few times before. And one is left with such gratitude and wondering: who pays them? Only you realise, they are always you and you know you better than you know yourself and it is their joy to assist you assisting themselves.

—

"My friend Daryl in energy form, arrives by my right side, and is expectant and waiting. He sometimes appears in energy form, and it has been common for me to experience people I know in something of a higher version of themselves, some sort of avatar.

A portal then opens from another dimension, with streaming ribbons of thick filaments of blue radiant light swarming into the earth and around me. A being of quicksilver blue, of masculine appearance, comes down and lands on my stomach area: 2nd chakra. He is very quick and timeless, flooding blue light and knowledge from where he is from, into this red pentness, of Mayan chambers of unconnected keeping of secrets. He is using something like a flashlight and a drill and he almost looks like a dentist high on nitrous.

When he is done, I ask him, What has he done? What does that mean? And he quickly turns as he leaves, showing a sign on himself, reading: "BE". I breathe silently and then go outside and smoke a cigarette in silence, and I say to my friend Shakti, "Most people wouldn't be smoking at this point" as reality was swirling around to the point where I could barely orientate myself at all.

Psychoactive Plants Around the World

The two primary classes of psychoactive chemicals found in plants are phenethylamines and tryptamines. The predominant psychoactive phenethylamine is mescaline, most commonly found in many cactus species in North and South America. There do not seem to be other phenethyl-amines found in nature that have the same potent psychoactive effect as mescaline. Peyote, for example, contains mescaline as its predominant alkaloid, as well as many other less potent alkaloids, many of which are phenethylamines.

DMT is the predominant psychoactive tryptamine in nature. Whereas much less common is 5-MeO-DMT, which is obtained from the Virola tree by some tribes in Amazonia, and often used in psychoactive snuff, but most commonly found as a pure synthetic compound in the West. Magic mush-rooms primarily contain psilocybin (O-phosphoryl-4-hydroxy-N,N-dimeth-yltryptamine), that is essentially DMT with a phosphorous atom on the four position, which means that the body does not recognise it as easily as DMT. Because DMT is an endogenous alkaloid, meaning the body already produces DMT, the body recognises DMT immediately, and so knows how to break it down very quickly with monoamine oxidase enzymes. Whereas the body does not easily know how to break down psilocybin when it is tak-en orally, typically allowing an experience to last four to six hours. The use of mushrooms and other plants such as morning glory, datura, and salvia in Central America is well documented. South America with its Amazon basin has the largest known culture of psychoactive plants – ayahuasca being only the tip of a very large iceberg of many largely undocumented and unresearched plants known to different Amazonian cultures.

Acacia trees and Syrian rue can grow side by side in the Middle East, and are often the only two plants growing in some regions. Combining Syrian rue that contains MAOIs like harmaline with acacias containing DMT can permit a strong oral DMT experience. Plants that appear to be acacia and Syrian rue are used as a Sufi initiation in Iran, according to a Sufi-initiated friend, and likely in other parts of the Middle East and indeed the world. The same friend has participated in two Sufi circles in Iran where this con-coction is taken in silence, while the partakers sit in a circle and journey deeply together. Another psychedelic researcher friend has communicated to me that he witnessed young Israelis extract DMT from apparently sea-sonally active acacia trees in Israel.

It is my understanding that psychoactive plants are used throughout the African continent; however, very little research has been carried out there. In the centre of Africa is the world's second largest rainforest, which is sure to be a repository of profound plant wisdom, but also within the borders of countries like the Democratic Republic of Congo, known to be one of the trickiest and most dangerous countries in which to travel.

The continuing problem for researchers in this field is that the use of psychoactive plants is often maintained a secret only accessible to the initiated. The traditional sacredness of such plants means that they are often tied up in tradition and cultures of secrecy. Also, it is often that the plants themselves do not simply want to become sold on the internet and available to 15-year-old kids who want to get 'fucked up'.

In Australia, the use of psychoactive plants is well reported and is known by some to be secret business among the Indigenous people. The understanding of the usage of these sacred plants is not something that the aboriginal people of Australia have necessarily been too keen to share with their white colonial invaders. Yet, I have spoken to dozens of aboriginal and non-aboriginal people who have revealed a lot of anecdotal information about the use of psychoactive plants. One informant of mine was an aboriginal initiated man who was compelled to tell me that his initiation involved taking a combination of plants (which included Acacia) that worked at the strength of smoked DMT, but instead of lasting ten minutes, lasted three days!

Additionally in Asia, the use of psychoactive plants has been reported. In Nepal, the shamans take psychoactive mushrooms, as reported by the German ethnobotanist Christian Rätsch. It is also well known that Tibetan Buddhist monks take powerful psychoactive plants in conjunction with advanced meditation practices. In nations like Indonesia and Thailand, I have heard reports of advanced herbal knowledge utilised for psychic and sexual activation.

In Europe, there are psychoactive plants of power that grow quite commonly, such as psilocybin-containing magic mushrooms and the *Amanita muscaria* or fly agaric mushrooms, as well as plants that most would consider to be of lesser potency, such as henbane or mandrake, which most modern day psychedelic explorers do forsake.

Lesser-known and much less commonly utilised plant psychoactives are Morning Glory and Hawaiian baby woodrose, which both contain Lysergic acid. Lysergic acid works in a similar way to LSD, by accessing the serotonin receptors. I have met few people who prefer LSA to high-quality LSD, so it certainly has its fans. The issue here is that unless picked very fresh, plants containing LSA will tend to result in weaker experiences than the ones catalysed by LSD.

Another psychoactive agent found in nature are fly agaric mushrooms (*Amanita muscaria*) – the large, red and white spotted mushrooms found throughout north Europe and Siberia, where shamans are known to use them. Western psychonauts have often been less interested in this mushroom, perhaps because of an absence of known traditions surrounding them, and perhaps because their effects are not as well known as that of other visionary plants. A few different friends have reported marvelous and incredibly powerful effects from the mushroom known as *Amanita muscaria*, with a few swearing of its immense value and power. However, *Amanita* needs to be carefully prepared, which normally means extensive drying in an oven or in the sun, so that the toxic ibotenic acid converts into muscimol.

Datura, and also plants of the *Brugmansia* genus, are well known to have a certain reputation for being strong psychoactive plants. Yet, far from being something to work up to, I found datura to make me so ill, that I didn't care about the visions, which reminded me of fever visions. I felt so bad I wanted to die, and so didn't really care about what I saw. What I did see and experience under the influence of this plant didn't impress me at all and I found nothing in it to warrant further ingestions. After talking to many people who have taken datura, I can say that very few find it useful and most, if they survive the potentially very messy and delusionary journey and even if they don't go blind for a time, say what they learn from datura is never to do it again!

Iboga and Ibogaine

Tabernathe Iboga is perhaps the most fascinating psychoactive plant known to the West, commonly known for its ability to detoxify addicts from heroin. If an opiate user tries to take heroin within two weeks of ingesting iboga root or its principal alkaloid, ibogaine, nothing will happen, as ibogaine resets the opiate receptors. However, I believe that iboga is most usefully taken for personal transformation and healing. When I first took iboga, the most evident aspect of its nature was its humour, and it communicated to me mostly via images, but also auditorily. Interestingly, the overall experience of taking iboga I found to be very similar to taking ayahuasca on the third day of a week-long 'dieta' deep in the Amazon rainforest, where I experienced a total communion with the spirit of ayahuasca.

Many feel that iboga is inherently tied into traditions based in Gabon, a country in West Africa. From talking to people who have been there to take iboga with the Bwitists, I would have to say that this environment does not sound like one in which to have the most conducive experience with the plant. Friends have reported being distracted by the ritual itself of people dancing and singing and shaking them every five minutes, and also say they felt they were treated by the locals as a walking ATM machine in that country.

Besides that, traveling to South America is one thing, but shysters appear even more prevalent in Gabon, than in a country such as Peru. People should also understand the amount of iboga given for an initiation experience can be dangerously high. The initiation dose of root bark is often so high that initiates have been known to die. People in Gabon generally only take iboga once or twice in their lifetime at this quantity. Furthermore, the types of experiences one can have with high dosages of iboga are ultra-cosmic, but they may not be really relevant to the human lifetime of the person taking the iboga. I believe a good, 'full flood' dosage of strong iboga root bark (4 - 6% alkaloids) is in the order of 10 to 20 grams, rather than two or even three times that amount. At this sort of dosage, the plant as healer and teacher really comes to the fore, and this is where a lot of healing work can occur. Dosages of 5 to 10 grams are also extraordinarily useful, and many people around the world are facilitating iboga groups with this sort of dose of Iboga root bark.

Iboga is a plant that many people are scared of, but essentially, I think they are scared of facing what the iboga will reveal about themselves. Iboga is not there to hit anyone over the head with a two-by-four plank because it is malevolent, but only because it feels certain forms of 'tough love' will wake the human up from their unconsciousness. Having said that, I have always felt iboga to be gentle and insightful – it just doesn't pull any punches telling the truth and is prepared to communicate the 'brutal' truth. I have taken iboga four times now at a dose of around 15 - 20 grams, once every two years, and for me, this 'full flood' dose is a completely friendly and healing experience. Each time I have taken iboga I have taken it by myself, although I would recommend that beginners take it with a sitter. Some people may need help to be able to go to the toilet, as it can be very difficult to walk under the influence of iboga. Iboga can also be very hard on the body. It is typical that people take certain tests to ensure they can endure how it will affect their heart and body when taking a strong dose and some people may be completely allergic to Iboga. The initial psychoactive experience of iboga is only about 6 to 12 hours, but it is likely that only on the fourth or fifth day after taking it will you be able to safely drive, and it really takes about a week or so to feel back to normal. Also, it is not guaranteed that the iboga spirit will really come to the fore every time with every person, and show them the visions and the visual data. Sometimes the experience will just be of feeling immobile, wiped out and unwell for some days. And yet, the Iboga still carries out its healing work.

I have yet to try the extracted compound ibogaine isolated from iboga, but if my experience with other plants is anything to go by, I would say that many of the other alkaloids in iboga root bark are also very beneficial and useful. I have also tried a tincture from iboga and found it to be half as strong as taking the powdered root bark in gelatin capsules. It seems that eating the actual root bark is necessary to garner the most from the plant and some people have taken to eating 1 - 3 grams of root bark with an extract of the total alkaloid profile in order to make a more essential contact with this 'wood'. Another fascinating aspect of iboga is how little is required to effect change in people. Taking tiny little amounts from a few milligrams of iboga works as the most incredible medicine for the mind and emotions. When 'micro-dosing' iboga, up to a few hundred milligrams can be taken and most people will gain a great deal from making contact with this most benevolent plant spirit.

An experience with iboga in Bali, July 2013

It wasn't so strong this time. The iboga was not quite so fully enveloping me, but it was strong enough. It shows me my brain and how it finds its way in and does what it needs to do, to do the holographic healing work it does.

Its healing work felt more like a scrub of various parts of my being that looked more like kitchen appliances than physical flesh. It showed me how it gets in there, twirling and shaking behind all these structures, like the ultimate dentist drill!

This time I felt more like the plant wanted to teach me than heal me. Its movements, its sounds and what it evokes are so detailed, complex and full of such artistry and for lack of a better word, humanity! What was it teaching? I think the same thing all psychedelics show us – to perceive the real we must let go of the apparatus of viewing the world through the comparative fog of our thoughts. So it is showing me many nuances, corners, angles and dimensions whereas, my mind feels like some planks frozen at 90-degree angles.

In the end it showed me a book stacked on top of a pile among many other stacks of books. The book had an intricately bound cover, the pages were open and I witnessed the most incredible text I had ever seen. The highly refined text moved, with little articulations in each letter twirling and switching. The text looked more like musical notation than writing and it was written in hand! Shapely gaps appeared and disappeared like invisible fingers blocking the view of the text and passing over the lines. The iboga then told me with great poignancy, reminiscent of the ultimate stillness, as if all things had been complete, that this book was my life.

Chapter Four

Ayahuasca

Introduction to Ayahuasca

Ayahuasca is the Quechua word for a vine known to Western people by its most common Latin name, *Banisteriopsis caapi*, historically used by many indigenous Amazonian tribes for shamanism, sorcery, divination, and healing. For those who drink ayahuasca, the vine is often perceived as a plant spirit that engages the mind, body, and spirit into a dialogue of personal understanding and healing.

The primary ingredient in an ayahuasca brew is the vine *Banisteriopsis caapi*, commonly revered as the mother of all plants. Other plants are added to the vine brew, typically those containing DMT, such as *Psychotria viridis* or *Diplopterys cabrerana,* and also many other plants not containing DMT, called admixtures, whose capacities are considered to be activated by the ayahuasca vine. In the Amazon, there is no traditional understanding of the existence of DMT per se, just that adding DMT-containing plants such as *Psychotria viridis* will give the ayahuasca brew more 'light' and visionary depth. Yet, the vine is considered to be the primary component of the brew, and the DMT-containing plants and other plants are typically considered to be admixtures to the vine brew. It is possible to drink a strong brew containing only ayahuasca vine and still experience a visionary state, although DMT containing plants are normally required for stronger visionary states.

In my experience, the thicker and older vines have an entirely different quality than the younger ones, and the thicker vines may well be over 100 years old. There are over 100 types of ayahuasca vine, and it is quite dramatically different in its effect depending on the strain and where the vine comes from within the Amazon basin, whether that is Peru, Brazil, Colombia or Ecuador. Clearly the effects of ayahuasca are due to much more than the differing combinations and ratios of chemicals called MAO inhibitors – harmine, harmaline, or tetra-hydroharmine – although inexperienced people will generally not understand this.

In the Amazon, many different admixture plants are brewed with the ayahuasca vine, and ayahuasca is considered to be an activator of all plants. Traditional healers known as 'curanderos' in the Amazon 'diet' with certain plants in order learn from them. The curandero communicates with the plants by ingesting and also contemplating on them. Ayahuasca is often considered a medium for understanding the healing power and other special teachings of the incredible range of plants in the Amazon, and indeed on earth.

What ayahuasca can do for you is entirely based upon where you are at in your development and your life. Many people experience communicating with and being guided by the ayahuasca spirit. Ayahuasca sometimes simply doesn't become visionary, especially when individuals first begin to drink it. It may take three times, or even 12 times or more until there are truly visionary effects beginning to be present for the neophyte ayahuasca drinker. In this circumstance, it is often said that there are obstacles preventing the brew from working that are being dealt with by the ayahuasca.

It would not at all be accurate to call ayahuasca a 'drug', because ayahuasca is not a drug, it is a vine containing beta-carboline alkaloids which facilitate the potentials of other plants, some of which contain DMT. Yet, you can get very high on ayahuasca. I have talked with people from the Santo Daime church for whom ayahuasca is their sacrament, who celebrate how high you can get drinking ayahuasca. Of course, being high is not a bad thing. It is I think, a negative trait of puritanical western culture to dismiss the sheer pleasure of enjoying such communion. That being said, there are very few people who are going to drink ayahuasca and feel like they have snorted cocaine or smoked crack, as the resulting state is not so immediately pleasurable. You normally have to drink a foul brew, as the well-known author Graham Hancock accurately describes as tasting like "old socks, raw sewage, sulphur, battery acid and chocolate". Then, after drinking this stomach-churning concoction, the imbiber is very likely to become nauseous and vomit it up.

Graham Hancock further reports:

"But after the vile taste has faded, and even while I'm still enduring the horrible physical side effects, I find myself spirited away to an enchanted universe. There, like Rick Strassman's volunteers in the DMT research described yesterday, I encounter intelligent beings that have teachings to impart to me. Often its lessons about myself, stuff in my life I need to fix, old habits that no longer serve me, love I need to learn to give better. But sometimes ayahuasca goes further and allows me to peep, or so I imagine, into the mysterious nature of reality, and shows me our planet as a haven of light and life, and teaches me that the jungle is sentient and sacred."

The ayahuasca visuals could be perceived as a kind of 'dreaming while awake', but this does not mean that the visions are normally much like the visual phenomena that occur in dreams. Ayahuasca visuals do not look like anything one typically experiences in dreams – the geometric patterns and the beings do not appear in the same way as in the dream state. Nothing as startlingly alien appears in dreams and dreams are much more metaphoric and symbolic, whereas the ayahuasca visions communicate quite directly.

There are people who judge those who go to Peru as ayahuasca tourists to partake of these types of visionary experiences as seekers simply wanting to be plugged into 'ayahuasca TV'. Interacting with these visions is enough for many people and a good beginning for the Western mind to accept these experiences as not just some delusions or 'hallucinations'. Of course, it is useful for many to understand that these experiences actually have validity, relevance, and meaning. It might take some people a few sessions to realise this, but in the end, I think most do.

Encountering archetypal beings or themes is quite impressive for many people. Archetypal beings or their representations appearing in the dream state is a phenomenon that Jung reported. As he reports in his book *Memories, Dreams and Reflections*, these archetypal beings would also sometimes appear to him in his daily waking consciousness. Many people who drink ayahuasca will often communicate with archetypal beings such as the Indian deity Ganesh, and it is almost as common for people to meet archetypal beings as alien beings – although you do hear of different people meeting similar sorts of alien beings, 'octopus woman' being one that I have heard from different people that they have experienced.

The Religion of Ayahuasca

So what are the contents of an ayahuasca experience? Benny Shanon, in his book *Antipodes of the Mind*, does a very good job describing the different types of experiences people can have with ayahuasca. As a newcomer, what will most likely occur is a theme of events that have been experienced by other people, often many times. There can be profound experiences of illumination that some may mistake for a kind of enlightenment, or the very palpable experience of getting your arse kicked! Of course, mindset and physical setting have much to do with what one experiences. One of the most profound aspects of the ayahuasca experience is simply that of letting go, releasing control, facing one's fears and going deeply within.

What is the purpose of drinking ayahuasca? Of going through the ordeal of drinking a vile brew and then throwing it up? For many, the aim is to become proficient in these areas of beingness. For some it is to gain self-understanding and to work through particular issues in their lives, to heal and learn from the plants. Others are aiming to carry out particular learnings from plants and/or other beings. From the plant's perspective, ayahuasca is mostly focused on healing and carrying out an inner work that affects many different levels of the human being. And what if you don't want to do the inner work? Well, that is like going to a psychiatrist and saying you don't want to talk – except in this case, the plant has you cornered, because you are completely within its domain.

The vomiting aspect of ayahuasca is a purging and a clearing. Even those who do not normally enjoy vomiting typically enjoy the ayahuasca purge. Most people who partake of ayahuasca want to release their shit and surrender their vomit, and yet many take ayahuasca under conditions resembling a guided meditation. Some in the West take ayahuasca, sing bhajans (Sanskrit chants) and rainbow songs, and wear white. Personally, this sort of 'scene' has never appealed to me.

The primary reason people drink ayahuasca in groups is because traditionally, in Amazonia, people come to the curandero for physical healing. In a group, the curandero can give ayahuasca to many people at the same time and perform healing for them, or he/she may not give them ayahuasca at all and only take the ayahuasca themselves in order to more effectively perform healing. What has occurred in the last few decades, especially for Westerners, is the development of taking ayahuasca in groups for the purpose of experiencing its visionary qualities. These groups congregate because the plants are not always easy to get, most do not know how to prepare and brew the plants, and there are no ayahuasca dealers. But perhaps most of all, people do not feel confident drinking such powerful medicine by themselves, or at least without supervision from someone with more experience and understanding than themselves. Having said this, drinking alone is often preferable for many people who feel drawn to journeying deeply with ayahuasca. And it is often the case that groups in the West can contain a large number of people, often squished together, with some participants making a great deal of noise. Many in the West stress the ritual leader or the idea of being guided. For whatever reason, the Western mind believes very much in ceremony, in 'ritual'. Perhaps this is because such rituals and ceremonies were historically encountered in Western European society a couple of thousand years ago, before the Romans and the Christians largely forced their religion onto pagan Europeans, and so the knowledge of such rituals has largely been lost. It could be said that this desire or need for ritual in modern day Western people speaks of a kind of primal desire to reconnect with their European indigenous culture. In Western society, the most common forms of communal ceremonies or rituals are carried out by modern day Pagans, Christians, Satanists, and Masons. The ceremony or ritual is perhaps something of a focalising glue or container for the communal nature of the group. Because the ceremony is the element that fulfills a profound sense of belonging, it is held in very high esteem as the primary element which allows this communion and fellowship between human beings.

Perhaps this ideology of the necessity of ceremony and ritual occupies the Western mind, because the traditional indigenous European ceremonies of thousands of years ago have been lost and there is a something of a nagging sense that these rituals must be re-enacted. Yet, I think the plants are more interested in being present to us in raw simplicity, nakedness, and communication, all of which seems to confront the Western psyche, which is seemingly addicted to the need for control and the strict social conformism our particular form of 'civilisation' apparently demands.

In the formal carrying out of a ceremony, certain physical actions may represent a serious expression of intent. Although, if we get stuck on taking those actions, it is possible to lose the intent and end up only performing rote actions. It seems to me that ritualised forms of ayahuasca sessions or 'ceremonies' may often prevent the full potential of the experience. Even more so than the diet, it is human impositions, ideas, organisations, and rules that I think really prevent an enlivened and integrated spirit from coming through the individual and the group. Typically, what we are seeing in modern day ayahuasca groups – especially in the West, but also in South America, is a male 'shaman' who often appears to be trying to steal the show from the plant in order to demonstrate and show off his value in the 'ceremony'.

So much of the intentionality of these male shamans is very clearly directed by the same old profane trifecta of money, sex, and power – rather than a clear and pure intention to share the plants with other people, in order to enjoy and benefit from the richness of such sharing, communion and healing. Rather than the drinking of ayahuasca primarily being about the plants and the immense psychological, emotional, and spiritual work that can occur, these sessions often become focused on the performer and his guidance, his wisdom, his songs, and his cultural associations. Many curanderos often carry out the distribution of ayahuasca medicine as if what they are doing is more important than what is in the cup. I've come to feel that part of the prevailing epidemic of weak ayahuasca in the west, where people often tell me they need 3 to 4 cups to experience significant visionary effects, may well be due to the plants reticence to come forward, when they are deemed to be playing 2nd fiddle to the shaman.

Perhaps the advantage of the Santo Daime church's method of drinking ayahuasca is that their way does stress the unity of the group rather than the performance and power of an individual to 'guide' the session. Although it is true that the Santo Daime way of drinking ayahuasca appears odd to many people (because of the Portuguese hymns, formal uniforms, and dancing in a circle for hours – often under bright fluorescent lights), I personally do not have anything against these ways of taking ayahuasca. Still, I do think it would be very useful if we were all to own up to our own unique possibilities and fears without necessitating recourse to an organisation, structure or individual. I myself find the deepest internal work occurs in letting go, in surrendering, in lying down – not sitting up or standing up and performing in a group ceremony.

Many people often seem to face profound ontological insecurity in these states. It is my belief we should give space for people to find their own way, their own grounding, to find their own intelligence, which is their own true security – rather than compelling them to hang their hat on the ideologies of structure and outer forms of control, or presumed "guidance". As soon as anyone is presumably guided, they are then giving up their own guidance systems and then becoming dependent on the guidance of another.

Many people are also afraid of facing themselves, their own soul, intelligence, and shadow nakedly. Many fear losing control of themselves and their mind, to really face their fears and go into the multitude of so many different levels of reality that can be very confronting to an individual's cultural programming. It is my view that losing control is a necessary part of surrender and healing, so that we can lose the fear of letting go, and then learn to take responsibility for ourselves when we are no longer only controlled by the mind. The fact is, most people's minds are already out of control in the first instance – and their minds are spinning with the madness of their thoughts, which are already like runaway horses!

A lot of people stress the 'no sex' or 'dieta' element (normally meaning not eating salt, sugar, meat, and so on) in ayahuasca quite persistently. It is said that the primary reason the dieta exists is because the vine is jealous of men (mostly) giving their attention to other women. But also, within the context of a dieta, it is a commitment to give up certain things that show the plant spirits that you are serious. However, the contraindications against eating certain foods before drinking ayahuasca is largely a Western invention, related to food contraindications which may only be relevant for certain types of synthetic MAO inhibitors developed in the 1950s. That being said, before drinking ayahuasca I advise people to abstain from alcohol, drugs and foods high in tyramine such as red wine, blue vein cheese, and fermented foods. I know two people who had very serious health complications from drinking red wine 24 hours after and before taking a brew made with Syrian rue, which contains harmaline as the primary MAO inhibitor. Because the MAO enzymes break down tyramine, excessive amounts of tyramine in the human body can cause a very unpleasant 'hyptertensive crisis', which is caused by very high blood pressure.

For the drinking of ayahuasca over only one night, restraint from sex is not absolutely necessary. Sex is not necessarily draining and can often be energising, depending on the individual and their particular sexual framework. Then again, if individuals do feel they are involving themselves in a sexual framework which is draining, or that they are enmeshing themselves heavily in the energies of other people in a negative sense, then they may want to abstain from sex before ayahuasca. On that note, neither is strict adherence to the diet necessary for one-off drinking of ayahuasca and neither is any kind of fasting at all necessarily beneficial. I personally encourage people to eat healthily and lightly and relatively normally before drinking ayahuasca, as do many curanderos in Peru. There are curanderos in Peru who have given ayahuasca drinkers roast chicken before drinking. Ayahuasca drinkers in the

West can tend to be rather too earnest and serious, and may go over the top with their rules and prescriptions. As Buddha taught, an ascetic attitude can often represent a string that is tuned so tightly you cannot get a sound from it.

Ayahuasca has many incredible and largely unexplained benefits for humans. I have not experienced or heard of any plant or herb that has the ability to do so much good for the human body. I believe that many will eventually come to understand and appreciate ayahuasca's primary value as a medicine of the body and soul, rather than just as a facilitator of cosmic visions. It is very common for people to drink ayahuasca and have all kinds of muscle pains and ailments suddenly leave them due to its powerful healing effect. It is also very clear to me that ayahuasca has incredible anti-aging properties, and the youthfulness of ayahuasca drinkers is something that can often be observed. I think that more and more people will increasingly understand that a vine heavy brew, with relatively low amounts of DMT, is about the best preventive medicine a human being can ever take.

I do think that many put the ayahuasca spirit on a pedestal, making it like a deity, a god, or goddess talked about in sacrosanct tones. Ayahuasca has become something of a religion or the sacrament of a religion for many in the West, for whom ayahuasca is the centrepiece of their spirituality. Suddenly such individuals can access powerful states or realms in the spirit world not previously available to them and ayahuasca has become for them a true communion, a means to access an authentic spirituality.

My conclusion, after over a decade of seriously working with this plant and the states it induces, is that maybe we should not be too concerned about the spirit world and spirit beings after all. I do believe the states of consciousness ayahuasca can show us are beneficial to understand. But ayahuasca is hard work! Access to these worlds and visions often come at a price that many appear slow to completely understand. With ayahuasca there can also be an amplifying effect of the ego that can make the individual feel very important and special. Suddenly, one is carrying out superhuman work, doing superhuman deeds, and awakening into superhuman powers that can become very seductive to the ego. But such 'shamanic' work will not necessarily make you happy, fulfilled, or more loved by others or fulfilled in yourself. On the other hand, we live in a very troubled world that could do with more individuals engaging in serious shamanic work, working in the realms of the collective human psyche for the cause of the healing, awakening and evolution of humanity.

I do believe ayahuasca can be a very useful adjunct to personal work, but I don't treat it as the centrepiece of my spiritual life. I cannot say I am that absolutely compelled by the experiences I have with ayahuasca these days. Once you have seen the sights and had the delights many, many hundreds of times, they are no less enchanting, but there is no thirst or necessity anymore. Traveling to other countries can be especially enriching, but I cannot say that traveling to other countries is the primary purpose of life, even though I have traveled to 67 countries and consider the understanding and experiences involved in such traveling to be invaluable.

For me, ayahuasca and the plants have their most fundamental value in what they can do for my physical body and also bio-energetic body. This action of the ayahuasca is a non-visual, kinesthetic effect that one can become attuned to. Although these effects may initially appear subtle to many, these days I find this healing work to be the most predominant experience I have when taking ayahuasca. Out of all the plants and herbs one can take for one's health and wellbeing, ayahuasca appears to be the most effective on every level – and this is exactly how ayahuasca is taken by tens of thousands of regular people in Amazonia, as a super tonic to protect against disease and to allow for good health. The drive to increase the DMT content in ayahuasca brews was largely instigated in the 1980s, when researchers such as Jonathan Ott and Terence McKenna went to the Amazon and could not find ayahuasca brews that would give them visions. DMT dosages that modern day ayahuascaros give to the gringos are in no way representative of the traditional usage of ayahuasca, where the visionary qualities of the medicine are respected, but not considered primary.

As a facilitator of ayahuasca sessions, a lot of what I communicate to people is not to be too concerned about 'the entertainment', but to allow the plants to do their work. What changes afterwards is what is most important, and many people will notice profound shifts in their way of being. Ayahuasca is a true medicine for the mind, the body, and the soul, but it is not any sort of panacea. Many people will not find the healing they are looking for from ayahuasca and many people will not find the kind of spiritual content they are seeking. Others, however, will find what they are seeking and much, much more.

I do not believe in a dependence on this plant for its visionary qualities or for psychological or emotional healing. Generally, I would say the spiritual healing you can receive from other human beings is just as potent and often more relevant than that from ayahuasca. Of course, many people who facilitate ayahuasca groups do combine their spiritual healing work with the drinking of ayahuasca, which can be especially powerful.

The data of daily life is normally quite rich enough if we choose to open ourselves up to it, admittedly not always an easy thing to do. We don't need to traverse where ayahuasca can take us to be sustained or enriched in life. That being said, I have seen how ayahuasca has helped me and many others to truly live their lives. I could not imagine life without the incredible work it has done for me, and I do believe the ayahuasca group is an extremely valuable ritual form. In this place of coming together and supporting each other in a confrontation of self and being, a wonderful and magical space can be experienced.

How I facilitate Ayahuasca Groups

I always say that the smaller the ayahuasca group, the better; but realistically four or five people are the most intimate and comfortable number of people. With any more than 12 people the space tends to become much less intimate, and anything above 15 people I find to be potentially problematic, with a lack of space in many indoor venues, and then the amount of noise that number of people can make or that several people can make if they are going into deep processes. Larger groups can be very powerful and may be necessary at times, but it can be difficult for the participants to really get to know each other, and there can be a lack of intimacy in these larger groups.

I prefer to conduct sessions outside when the weather is good, and always at night. If it is cold, we might build a fire, but this is optional. The choice to drink ayahuasca at night-time is because the visions are much stronger in the dark. The daytime also presents too many opportunities for focusing on the external world, and I prefer to encourage people to go within. I ask people to set up where they are comfortable and spread out over a space – very rarely will there be a circle. I don't encourage a circle, or the holding of space as a group circle with all participants sitting up and looking at each other. Although I have done that at times in the past, it is then too easy to be distracted by other people, so I do not encourage 'holding circle' in this way.

While people are gathering and becoming comfortable, I try to be as informal as possible, making jokes and being naturally jovial. Normally, it is good to give people a couple of hours to meet the other participants and spend time setting up their own space. People naturally talk to one another, and I feel that putting everyone at ease is one of the most important things I can do as a facilitator. I do not believe in asking people to wear white as I am not convinced white is a preferable colour to wear, and I think people should dress in their own unique way and wear whatever clothes feel the most comfortable and practical to them.

At some point when everyone is ready, I will start talking. Normally, I do not make a big deal of rules. I believe that when human beings are told a bunch of rules, like children they will often unconsciously try to break them. I really try to give people a great deal of liberty and personal freedom, but also encourage respectful silence and remind participants to take care of one another. Two basic rules apply: try not to speak during the session, and try not to move out of the space and wander around too much. I will then typically talk about the plants in the brew, the nature of the brew, and what to expect from the experience. I will at times encourage people to make sound to guide their own experience, and if people have brought instruments I will let them know at what point in the session it may be appropriate for them to play. Then I will ask if anyone has questions and normally there are at least one or two.

Sometimes I will ask people to think about what they want out of the session. Most will have thought about this already, perhaps even for many years! I will then ask each person how deep they want to go – many people say they want a 'strong' brew. It is then a matter of knowing your plants well enough, in the ratios you have brewed them, to try and hit a 'sweet spot' for each person. Give them too much, and you may have people becoming very uncomfortable and possibly disturbing others by making too much noise. Give them too little, and they may not get as much out of the brew as they want.

When I first began to determine dosages of the brew for other people I used a pendulum, but these days my intuition and experience guides me. People with big body weights will usually need more brew and those of a certain hardened mental and psychic constitution will need more as well. On the other hand, sensitive, low body weighted, and receptive people will usually need less brew.

Then I will give them their cup and let them decide how they want to drink it, usually either slowly or down in one or more gulps. People are then free to talk to others about what the brew tastes like. Invariably there will be some people who like the taste and others who detest it. I may make honey available to take after drinking the brew and sometimes pieces of ginger, which can help with nausea. At this point, after people have drunk their brew, I will invite anyone who has a didgeridoo, guitar, or flute to play. Sometimes there will be people in the group whose focus is to play music. Sometimes half the people have brought instruments and will play them. Other times, I will play world music, electronic chill, classical, and world music of certain artists like 'Solar Fields' whose work I know is effective in the ayahuasca space.

After some time, I might go around smudging people with white sage or palo santo, a wood from South America traditionally used for clearing negative energies. Apart from this, there is no ceremony per se. The aim is to create a space as natural and comfortable as possible for the participants. Normally, things go pretty smoothly. Every so often someone panics and needs to be calmed down. Sometimes particular individuals can go through powerful processes that affect the whole group. Sometimes individuals need to be assisted if they are going through a difficult process. When this happens, I will often give bodywork, pressing certain pressure points (especially on the feet) to help the individual ground and surrender more deeply. Sometimes the person needs to be taken away from the group by a helper who will continue to support their journey away from the group if they are making noise and disturbing the other people too much.

For the most part, it all looks unexciting to outsiders, with a lot of people lying down and generally staying still. Some say that it is best to sit up and even more bizarrely, to keep one's eyes open, but I encourage the surrender of lying on the earth, rather than faux yogic control. When the session is peaking or about to peak, I will often turn the music off. At that point, people should be fully immersed so as not to need any music. The music is not for guidance, but for relaxation, comfort, and the pleasure of it in the space, as music sounds quite wonderful after taking ayahuasca. I much prefer listening to beautiful and diverse music than songs sung by a man of a particular style and type, which is what Amazonian icaros usually sound like to me.

When people are coming back from their experience, I will turn the music back on. At this point, people are usually quiet, and it can take some time for everyone to fully return. If a session started at 9 pm (which it very normally does), it will normally be around 2 or 3 am by this time. People will slowly begin to speak to each other and then go and get something to eat. Normally, I ask people to bring food to share – something simple like fruit, bread or soup. At this point, it is a good idea to get rid of the contents of the sick buckets if we are inside, as most people do tend to vomit. Often, there will be one or two other people helping with the session, and they will take away the vomit buckets and wash them down. Some people will just continue to lie down after the experience. Soon, most will want to go to sleep, and lying down right where they were is just fine. In the morning, people normally talk to each other and pack up.

A group debrief with each person taking turns sharing can be very useful and a much more open and honest space than most people are used to experiencing. Oftentimes, I will stay around until midday or the early afternoon in the space where we drank and converse with people there. It is also important to realise that with ayahuasca, the plant is still working in subtle ways for at least 24 hours.

Dosages of Tryptamines and Beta-Carbolines

During my initial oral ingestions of tryptamines, I did not believe there was a major difference between the *Banisteriopsis caapi* (ayahuasca vine) and MAO inhibitors (technically termed beta-carbolines) like *Peganum harmala*, often called Syrian rue. But with experience, I found the differences between these two plants to be quite pronounced. The value of Syrian rue is that it can be quite transparent in its effects, whereas the ayahuasca vine can often determine the nature of the experience in quite a pronounced way. People will often experience the voice and guidance of the vine, whereas most people will not experience the voice and guidance of the rue. Using Syrian rue can be especially valuable, because the DMT-containing plants and their wisdom can really come to the fore. Although, when taking ayahuasca vine, you can definitely still experience the guidance and wisdom of the DMT-containing plant, but when taking the Syrian rue, deeply engaging with the wisdom of the DMT-containing plant is almost assured.

Another advantage to utilising the Syrian rue is that you are likely to be able to walk around, and you will often not be so focused on your body and involved in the purgative features people often experience with ayahuasca vine. This is not to say that rue is not purgative or cleansing, only that it is not so physically involved or body-focused. When taking rue, one is more likely to be able to traverse through different dimensions, whereas the vine can often keep you focused on bodily and psychological issues, and bring you back to your own healing.

I have also utilised a pharmaceutical MAO-inhibitor with orally ingested DMT, called moclobemide, which is typically prescribed for depression. But eventually I came to feel it was not as beneficial as rue or ayahuasca vine. Most people who took it noticed a strange chemical feeling, and the experiences they provided were good, but after a time I came back to Syrian rue and ayahuasca vine, as the experiences they engendered were richer and seemed more useful to me. In my opinion and that of most others I know, pharmaceutical MAOIs like moclobemide should only really be considered a novelty item.

In Jonathan Ott's book, *Ayahuasca Analogues*, he talks of taking various combinations of beta-carbolines (MAO Inhibitors) and tryptamine-containing plants, and yet there is no clear sense as to the nature of his experiences. Without an understanding of what the meat and meaning of his so-called subjective experiences are, it is hard to gauge what is actually occurring for him at all. Based on chemical analysis of traditional ayahuasca brews, Jonathan Ott surmises that for a standard oral ingestion of MAO inhibitors and tryptamines, 150mg of harmine is required along with 30-60 mg of DMT in the preparation of an 'ayahuasca analogue'.

Modern day researchers, spearheaded by people such as myself, have realised that Jonathan Ott's calculations fall short of what most explorers need for a truly visionary experience. Even with a strong harmine/Banisteriopsis caapi dosage, 30 - 60 mg of DMT is not sufficient to produce significant visionary effects in most people. This may well be the amount of DMT taken in truly traditional, very vine-heavy ayahuasca brews in the Amazon – but traditional ayahuasca brews taken by Amazonian people are not normally taken for their visionary effects, but for the health-giving and healing effects of the ayahuasca vine. Also, in many traditional ceremonies people will take many cups of ayahuasca over a night, and traditional Amazonian people are likely to need less DMT to bring them into visionary states than people of western european descent. And furthermore, the brews are often so vine heavy as to present side effects such as severe nausea, heaviness or inabilty to move. With these very heavy doses, 30 - 60mg of DMT may be visionary for some people. Although, it is very common for me to hear of people drinking with indigenous people, which I have done so myself a few times, and experience very little in the way of visions.

So in fact, a dosage of 30 - 40 mg of DMT is where tryptamine-like effects just begin to occur for most people, and 10 - 25 mg DMT is not really noticeable above the gentle psychoactive effects of the harmine. Each person is different and for some rare individuals, 30-40 mg may be about as much DMT as they wish to take – but most people need at least 60 - 80 mg for sufficient psychoactive effects and even at this dosage, you generally cannot expect a full-blown visionary experience, even when using a strong dose of 4 grams of syrian rue or 100 grams of strong *caapi* vine. Also, it should be pointed out that going beyond 4 grams of syrian rue (around 200-280mg of harmaline) or 100 grams of strong *caapi* vine (150-250mg of harmine) can increase the negative effects of these beta-carbolines - which include a feeling of heaviness, pressure in the head, inability to walk properly, more purging and perhaps more of an emphasis on bodily processes.

An oral dosage of 100 mg of DMT is where the visionary qualities really begin to occur, for most people say when they are taking 3 grams of Syrian Rue or 80 grams of strong vine, and in context, 40 - 60 grams of strong vine is enough to fully MAO inhibit most people. More like 150 mg of DMT is a good standard, strong tryptamine experience. For many, 200 mg is necessary for the DMT to be vision- potent in a way that puts them in a place where they feel they are receiving the data they require. For some, that amount of DMT may be 300 mg, or even up to a half a gram or 1 gram in very rare individuals, but 300mg is the uppermost end of what most people would want to ingest. I would say to neophyte explorers to tread carefully, and to slowly increase your DMT dosage in increments: perhaps starting at 60mg, going to 100mg, then 150mg, and finally to 200mg or more. Some people are going to find 100 - 200mg of DMT to be exceedingly strong, and it will perhaps give them an experience they did not feel ready for. It is also that, many first timers are going to need more DMT to break through into a visionary state, because of their defences and resistances, meaning that first timers may require implausible amounts of medicine in the beginning to have visionary experiences, while after those defences and blockages have been worked through, they will normally need less. Whereas, more experienced explorers who have sensitised themselves to the state, are going to need less and less DMT over time. I know one lady who only needs to have one small sip of Ayahuasca to have a full blown visionary experience.

It came to my attention after an embarrassing number of years, that taking freebase crystal DMT orally was not as potent, colourful, or clear as taking the equivalent amount of DMT in a tea that was brewed from the plant. For many years, I couldn't see how there could be a difference, but after doing some comparisons, it was obvious that the tea was much better, and the experiences resulting from the crystalline extract were inferior. You could take twice or even three times as much DMT crystal as the equivalent in brew, and the experience from the crystal would never be as bright or full as that from the tea. Why could this be? When extracting DMT, chemicals like sodium hydroxide and liquid petrochemical hydrocarbon solvents are commonly used. In this chemical extraction process, it would appear that some dimensions and qualities of the tryptamine molecules are compromised. Also, there is the factor of isolating the alkaloids from the rest of the plant. For example, there are very few people who say that extracted pure mescaline from the cactus is as potent or full bodied compared to when they take the dried powder or tea made from the cactus flesh.

When making a tea from the whole plant, you are extracting the essence of the plant intelligence from its very flesh, not just isolating the alkaloids. In the alchemic method 'Spagyrics' developed by Paracelsus, often considered the father of modern medicine, the ashes of the plant are commonly burnt and then blended back into an alcohol-extracted tincture. Friends who have experimented with this procedure report that a Spagyric tincture of ayahuasca is much more potent than a normal tea prepared from the same amount of ayahuasca vine.

Ayahuasca leaf can technically be used to make ayahuasca brews, but does not tend to carry the brew, or really 'take' the ayahuasca drinker on a solid journey, just as thicker and older vine tends to carry the brew much further than younger and thinner vine. Many people will not know the difference, but I find that the older, thicker vine will allow me to travel to certain places and bring through certain sounds and frequencies that are just not possible with younger and thinner vine.

I have used many DMT-containing Australian acacias with ayahuasca and can say that many of the acacia species work exceptionally well when combined with the ayahuasca vine in the tea. Some people say that Ayahuasca containing Australian acacias cannot be considered Ayahuasca. I personally do not understand that, as Ayahuasca is normally considered the primary component and the DMT containing plants are considered to be admixtures. I actually very rarely use Amazonian DMT containing plants, and much prefer the spirit of the Australian Acacia trees. Of course, a brew containing Australian Acacia as the DMT source is completely different to an Ayahuasca brew containing Amazonian DMT sources.

It is also possible to include small amounts of admixture plants, which do not contain DMT into the brewing process, but are combined for their possible medicinal and/or spiritual qualities. Many of these admixture plants can also teach, heal and communicate to people when they are added to an ayahuasca brew. I would recommend a great deal of caution to people who wish to use admixture plants not traditionally utilised in Amazonia – as many plants have an unpredictable effect when combined with the ayahuasca vine, and so I would advise explorers in this field to tread carefully. It is certainly useful to open up a dialogue with the plants you wish to utilise as an admixture and to be wary of their potentially immense and unpredictable power when activated by the Ayahuasca vine.

People talk about the possibility of an ayahuasca pill, and it is technically feasible to create such a thing – but as the pill would be an extract of isolated DMT and MAO inhibitors, I don't think the experience could ever be as full or rich as taking a pure plant-based liquid brew. I know many will say these are my own prejudices, but I think this becomes clear to most as they work with the plants and become more sensitive and aware of their effects. Many people claim (often quite arrogantly and with unwarranted certainty based on very limited experience) that such apparent differences in effect are merely subjective and superstitious. But as stated previously, what we are doing is carrying the plant intelligence into a form that can connect with the human being. Of course, you can still have powerful experiences when you isolate the alkaloids, but the potential range, breadth, and richness will fall short in comparison to a brew. After some years of working with the plants, I think you become sensitive to different concoctions, and the differences between different brews becomes very evident. You develop a palate which can ascertain the many different 'tastes' and qualities of the constituents of brew, just like wine tasters have the ability to ascertain subtle qualities and flavours in wine.

When it comes to utilising Syrian rue, I prefer to make a brew rather than take a harmala extract, to experience the fullest and brightest effects. Harmala extracts can, however, provide a clear and smooth experience, but they can also lack the noticeable uplifting pulse and vigour that you can get from a good Syrian rue brew. Different batches of Syrian rue work differently – some are stronger and fuller, some are brighter. Some of these brews made from Syrian rue will be like a fine, full-bodied and sophisticated wine – while other brews will be like some cheap red wine! I have tasted fresh Syrian rue from seeds in Jordan, and after taking two seeds from the pod sublingually, I noticed mild psychoactive effects. I have also had Syrian rue that may have been languishing in stockpiles for a decade or more at the Persian grocery store that left me feeling listless and depressed.

When brewing with plant matter, is fresh best? I would have to say that there is no major difference between fresh or dry. If you can handle what often may be a stronger taste, a brew made from fresh DMT containing plants can give somewhat brighter and light-filled visions. At the end of the day, I doubt that most people would be able to tell the difference between fresh and dry, as the experience is normally so profound anyway. When brewing with ayahuasca vine, fresh vine can be quite challenging for the body and can tend to create more nausea, although fresh vine can also provide a very fresh feeling. In no way have I ever found dry vine to be at all dead. I have found working with the vine somewhere in between fresh and dry, up to a month or so old (depending on storage conditions), quite satisfactory. It is useful to keep in mind when utilising the vine, that it can often 'take over' from the tryptamines. The experience is then mostly pertaining to the wisdom and communication of the ayahuasca rather than the particular admixture containing DMT. It is also possible that admixture plants, which do not contain DMT, can also take over the experience and come to the fore and communicate at times.

Two Ayahuasca Experiences

The following two reports are some of my own communications with the ayahuasca plant spirit.

January 2007, Melbourne, Australia.

When I was in England, a friend gave me some vine he had been keeping for a few years. It was 'cielo' vine, about the thickness of my wrist and curved like strange bones. My friend said this vine had been obtained by an infamous Englishman called Lord Sky Dancer, who had been given it from a very old shaman in the Peruvian Amazon. This vine traveled with me for some months in Europe until I had the opportunity to brew it up in Ibiza. There, I did two five-hour simmers on the vine, leaving it to soak for some time between each brew, and then simmered it right down using good-quality mineral water and small amounts of organic apple cider vinegar.

When back in Australia some months later, I ended up staying in the three-bedroom flat of a friend of my grandmothers, in probably the most exclusive suburb of Melbourne, and I wondered what drinking ayahuasca would be like in Toorak. At about 11pm I drank down 20 mls of vine by itself (about 170 grams of the dried vine). I knew from a previous experience that taking a lot of this batch was required to get significant effects. After drinking the brew, I rinsed my mouth right away with water, spat out the water, used some mouthwash, swished, and then spat it out and brushed my teeth! Still, it is funny how the bodily reaction to drinking ayahuasca is so strong, even though the mouth taste is largely gone quite soon if you follow this procedure.

I then inadvertently went to sleep at 11:15 pm and spontaneously woke up at 1:30 am (I had planned to take some DMT crystal at 11:45 pm). I then took the DMT, a transparent orangey crystalline extract from *Acacia obtusifolia*. I didn't have scales with me then, but it would have been around 130 milligrams or so, a relatively light dose for me.

I went to sleep again for 20 minutes, then woke up to a blonde woman in my visual field saying hello to me! The first thing I noticed was how different the DMT was or that in fact, what I was seeing did not look like DMT visions. What I was seeing, was the vine utilising the DMT in order to contact me. I had taken this same batch of DMT with another batch of vine recently, and now the visionary quality was totally different to the other experience. I could tell straight away that I was experiencing the field of intelligence of the vine and not the DMT from the acacia.

The images I then saw were very Peruvian, quite transparent and incredibly gentle. I saw monolithic-like land energies, smooth and clear with a fuzzy edge to them. The vine began talking to me in a male voice. I could actually hear it speak startlingly clear in my ears. It told me something of the shaman and how many things have recently changed where he lives, and then it said speaking English was quite hard. I laughed and said out loud how wonderful I thought that was.

The impression I had was of great humanity, a poignancy similar to communications in famous literature. I think we would do well to remember that there is actually a living plant out there this vine is connected to. Even the dried part of the plant can contact the individuated living intelligence of that specific plant, something akin to its soul.

Then it got to work and 'went' into my stomach first off. I could see it like a Peruvian labourer, going in and trying to pull up deep blockages there. It felt like old dead tree stumps were being uprooted from within my being. This took some time, and I could feel it really going in there. Eventually it pulled out this stuff that it showed me to be purplish black squares connected together like black goo that was just blocking energy. I got the impression that it came from one of my grandfathers, an energetic patterning passed down through the genetics, but I didn't really ask, and the vine didn't seem to think it was so important that I needed to know.

That was it really, and there was nothing much more to the experience and not much fallout, just a much lighter feeling in my stomach. Now at almost 5am the same morning, there was a very definite circulation of energy that wasn't there before, almost a sense of this new space in my system and a rebalancing, an opening of the body's energies.

I thought how this experience of being in communion with the vine is not the cosmic consciousness typical of the DMT-centered experience; it was very much a kind of horizontal, quite contained communion with a plant spirit. Also, I thought of how there is an orchestration, how this blockage is freed at this time, but not all blockages could be released at once as it takes time to assimilate and deal with the ramifications of freeing up stagnant energy within one's being.

A report from a week-long dieta in the Amazon in July 2006.

Two women friends and I traveled by riverboat 12 hours down the Rio Ucayali from Iquitios in Peru, and then took a canoe two hours down a tributary to a Matses village. We then walked five hours into the jungle (not too far from the Brazilian border) where we stayed in a crude open hut for a week, followed the dieta, and drank ayahuasca with a 75-year-old male curandero called Don Gallindo.

Our curandero was a maestro of admixture plants and I learnt how powerful ayahuasca is as a facilitator of the power of other plants, not just those containing DMT. During the first night drinking the ayahuasca, I could literally feel the other admixture plants rush through my system circulating and opening up my channels and pushing out obstructions, with much throwing up.

During the second experience, I journeyed deeper with the vine than I ever have. We achieved a gentle intimacy, and she performed a profound healing on my body and whole system, traveling to problem areas with gentleness, intelligence and precision. Just that demonstration of gentleness changed something in me. I could literally feel the soul of this particular vine in me and healing me from the inside. I have not experienced this mastery of healing in any human being, and I was forever changed by the eight-hour experience. I was given a song with a very simple and beautiful melody. I repeatedly told the plant that I was not able to remember melodies, but she played the tune more than half a dozen times! Via the plant spirits sharing melodies and songs, the shamans learn their icaros. These songs have come directly from the plants, and this is why icaros are considered to have the power they do.

So this particular vine communicated with me, showed me animations and movies, and such beautiful high art. It is interesting, because no human art or animation really comes close. I thought how mistaken people are in pedestalising this plant that in its own way is only a plant; in the same way that we are only human, and imperfect. Some of her perspectives I felt were rather harsh and uncalled for, and yet the playful soulfulness of the plant itself I have never received so clearly. It really does have a very sharing nature. I then understood why the shamans stress the dieta. It seems the plant itself has even requested a certain level of commitment to it, by this disciplined focus and gathering of energies, in order to allow the plant spirit engage with the body and mind.

All my sessions and all the times I have ever drunk ayahuasca have been powerful, but this experience was just the plant spirit working on me, which I think is the essence of ayahuasca healing. During previous experiences of drinking ayahuasca, the spirit of the vine has come in very obviously and carried out deep work, but mostly I felt it in my bones, in a general overview of deep work on the body and energy bodies, not so specific and direct as this experience was.

These experiences deep out in the Amazon were all about healing, and this is the most obvious business the plant has with us. That healing is first and foremost a mental, emotional and spiritual healing – an alignment to intelligence, to light, to love. The third time I drank, the first thing I saw was a jigsaw animation scrolling past me, with all its pieces together and locked in, clearly a sign of completion. The work with me had been completed this time! There was nothing more to work on right now. Our curandero Don Gallindo was a gentle man himself, and really did a fantastic job of putting himself aside and just being a pure facilitator for the power of the plants.

This vine definitely appears to be a female to me, with a certain kind of nurturing and supportive quality that humans normally interpret as feminine. A few months later, I had the occasion to eat a significant dose of iboga root bark, a highly potent African plant that was very clearly a male presence. Once again, the plant immersed itself into the energetic human structure and acted as a healer and facilitator of transformation, bringing with it what I can only describe as incredibly hilarious visionary cartoons. The iboga gave me the same experience of being fully immersed in the realm of the plant spirit carrying out deep and intense healing. I would say that iboga is deeper and more focused in this regard, yet perhaps less versatile than ayahuasca.

Chapter Five

Considering Other Beings

"But are the Beings Real?"

There are many different types of beings that people can meet in the psychedelic state, yet our cultural programs and literally our 'wildest dreams' do not admit that anything like these beings exist. What is clear to me and almost all of the people who have explored these states of consciousness extensively, is that these beings do exist in the way that they themselves say they do, and that all other explanations represent protestations of the 'rational' mind.

Sometimes, the presence of these beings represents the beginning of an initiation or process, or its culmination. Other times these beings seem to be assessing our state. Oftentimes, they want to meet you in order to teach and share wisdom. Much of the time, these beings seem to be performing a kind of work or surgery for the benefit of the human subject. The work they do may involve pulling 'things' from the body, or it can appear that they are adding computer-like components similar to 'chips' to the human technology. Some of these beings may be related directly to the individual, or they may appear to represent a higher evolutionary culmination of what a human being is. These beings may describe themselves in different ways, but normally the data they communicate is received visually rather than audibly, although many of these communications are of a telepathic, energetic or super-sensory nature. Sometimes, these beings may want to commune in different ways that may appear sexual to us. But actually, these communions may just represent the communication of energy, light or life force, and the intermingling and engagement of essence in relationship, in a way that normally has little to do with genital interaction. It is also possible to receive help from these beings, and of course it is possible to ask them questions and receive various types of assistance from them.

It is possible to meet all kinds of crazy critters and harlequin-like beings in many different cartoon-esque dimensions, like the beings that Terence McKenna often talks about. They will often show you sparkly toys and things that move around in clever ways, and their communications can become 'boring' and repetitious. Many of these beings can be entertaining, but nonetheless there is nothing absolutely captivating about these sorts of experiences. When taking psychoactive plants, it is easy to miss the fact that much of the time we are often just being entertained. Plants such as iboga and ayahuasca will quite often visually entertain the human patient while carrying out deep psychic work upon them. Perhaps this type of visual entertainment is an inbuilt impetus that exists in the natural world for the higher primates to reach for and continue to take these plant medicines?

Many years ago, I was engaging in deep inner work of a certain theme and process. Just before truly entering the intensity of the oral DMT space, I was presented with a male and female performance troupe that would appear in the air before me and show me elaborate tricks of themselves intertwining, bending, flexing, and melding into each other – as if it was the Cirque du Soleil from hundreds of years in the future! After they waved good-bye and left, the content of my experience became a lot more serious.

The beings that people can meet are many and manifold, and if you are experiencing some sort of 16-bit 'elves', then one can only assume you have smoked some shoddily manufactured synthetic DMT, and/or that you have not smoked enough! Because such so-called elves do not at all begin to express the manifold types of creatures that many do meet in the psychedelic state, particularly in the tryptamine state, whether through taking high doses of mushrooms, smoking DMT, or from taking ayahuasca.

Skeptically minded individuals may infer that these beings are some sort of projections of the brain or the mind, but why would the mind project these beings? What function would that serve? Is this the way the human mind wants to communicate with itself – by creating other forms entirely alien and different? This is a fundamental point, because these forms are typically so alien and entirely different from what the mind has seen before, that we have to ask: where would the mind get this kind of complex data from in the first place? Those like James Kent who contend that the content of DMT experiences could easily be reconstructed from memories, are basically only telling us they haven't really explored the extent and complexity of the DMT space.

Even if it is the case that the human mind could instantly generate these extremely sophisticated beings and the incredible art that can be experienced, the idea that DMT could give one an experience of one's mind communicating to itself is still, of course, very significant. Yet, there are very few people who have seriously explored this field who maintain this view. The most common sense conclusion, after working through the protestations of the 'rational mind', and after experiencing many visitations of profundity and absolute meaningfulness, is that these beings are what they say they are and should not be relegated by our 'rational' mind to be something other than what they say they are. It just doesn't make sense to try and explain these beings away. In fact, it comes off as a defensive tendency of the rational Western mind that wants to avoid looking foolish by not buying into apparently 'paranormal' phenomena. The existential uncertainty involved in accepting this material on its own terms can cause the Western mind to become highly insecure. Also, accepting this material on its own terms means potentially facing so much cognitive dissonance that the mind then rushes to find alternative explanations, when in this case, none will suffice that do not look ridiculous and inadequate.

Perhaps the most common sense, purely materialistic explanation for DMT visions, is that the brain manufactures these experiences because of a heightened processing power due to the presence of a more than usual amount of neurotransmitters. Even though many so-called materialists do experience startling, apparently separate and real beings, some will still maintain these beings are a kind of projection or 'hallucination' of the brain. It is quite interesting that some people, no matter how alien and strange the beings they see are, will still be absolutely adamant that it can only be their 'brain' they are seeing. Yet there are also many definitions of 'brain'. Timothy Leary would say "Your Brain is God", which is quite a monistic non-dual statement! But if you do see your brain as god, and god is defined as all that there is, then by that definition, your 'brain' could be all that you are seeing! Some say it doesn't matter where you think your experience comes from, because the experience itself is typically so extraordinary, transformative and potentially healing, that it is something of a moot point. I would disagree, and say that anachronistic, anthropocentric views or perspectives, which innately put the human at the centre of the world, represent an unnecessary reactionary inanity of 'flat earth' reductionist narcissism.

Does it truly make sense that the brain communicates precise wisdom or communication about how to live a better life, in the form of elaborately detailed dancing deities? If so, then I think this demonstrates the brain is a lot less mechanistic than modern day science typically understands it to be. If we are to look at the history of scientific understanding in the west, the trend over time is that there are paradigm shifts which contend that existence itself is much bigger and less anthropocentric than we have previously understood it to be.

The experience of smoked DMT often involves understanding directly that existence is much bigger than present human models of understanding typically give it credit for. People who maintain the present models of reality to be verdant truth, can only be expected to exist in any given time. Once again, I think the true value of smoked DMT is that it can show us directly that what we know of reality is much bigger and mysterious than anyone can truly conceive of. I think that those who say that what is "real" must conform to our present day models of reality, really are missing the point entirely. The point is, if there is to be growth of our present models of reality, there must be paradigm shifts which confront or challenge the inherent limitations of the present models of reality. If anything, I think it is important to be skeptical of all present models of reality and conveniently limited worldviews.

There are people who eschew the purely materialist version of reality, and consider all the magnificent and mysterious visions and beings to be some sort of imaginary manifestation of the human mind or consciousness. Such people may meet and talk to apparently other beings or plant spirits, but consider they are having conversations with themselves. Yet, ultimately, everything could be perceived to be consciousness communicating with itself, and hyperspace could be perceived as one big quantum singularity. And yet it consistently surprises me how some people are able to glibly dismiss the grandiosity and immensity of these experiences as a reflection of themselves or just as "imagination".

I can only say, that it might take smoking high dose DMT many dozens of times over some years to really gain a full appreciation of the breadth, power and depth of what can be experienced in the depths of these states. People who maintain these sort of fixed and limited positions might have only smoked DMT a dozen times, if that. I would say there normally comes a point in which surrender of the mental apparatus is the only choice, and the human mind has to admit that it cannot understand or interpret what is being experienced. However, some people have more developed minds than others, and the most apparently intelligent people are often those who maintain certain descriptions or understandings of the phenomena which assume some sort of understanding. These are also the people who may often need to put in the most effort to crack open their head, get out of the known, unfoolish mind, face their own cognitive dissonance, and go through the hard work of completely reassembling their world view, in the face of the truly ineffable, as many have done before them.

After some time experiencing the phenomena of other beings, the human mind often simply gives up trying to describe or explain it away. I used to say it took having the experience of meeting 667 beings before my rational mind simply gave up trying to explain what they were. It is then not a matter of belief, but direct experience, which is taken for granted. It is interesting to look into why people want to say that these beings are somehow an anomaly or artifact of brain functioning, when it clearly isn't any of those things! I think it is evident that the human mind under the influence of DMT reacts strongly to being confronted with the fact that it is truly not alone. Like the innately selfish baby human, it is confounded and confused that it is not the centre of the universe, especially in what it often deems to be a random and chaotic universe, from which its own intelligence seemingly sprang from genetic mutation and response to stimuli, all based purely in the realm of survival.

Theories and explanations of reality, such as Darwin's theory of evolution, allow many to understand and feel that they have understood that there is a single, definite description of our intelligence and life force. But I think these theories let us off the hook, as they allow us to believe that the case has been closed. Furthermore, such simple theories do not explain why there is consciousness, or the purpose of higher order functioning that does not relate to survival. Perhaps explanation in and of itself is not the point, and does not really further the explorative evolution of understanding. When one comes into contact with much more confounding and complex dimensions of existence than the one we typically inhabit, I think that explanation and even understanding become less relevant.

There are many things that can be shown to the human mind that it simply cannot comprehend, and realising this is liberating in and of itself. We are then released from the need to understand, because it is shockingly clear there is a deeper order of intelligence beyond us. But is this deeper order of intelligence God? Perhaps the tendency of many to constantly return to concepts of God trivialises the nature of existence itself. What we would see as any specific thing is simply embedded in an overall fractal, whereby, if we zoom in or out, there is simply more detail, more specifics, and more intelligence. But I think it is very clear that deep experiences with compounds like tryptamines do show us that there is an intelligence superior to that of the human species. This also liberates us from the arrogance that we owe life an interpretive understanding or comprehension of what is occurring. Often when coming back from a breakthrough DMT experience, much of what is experienced is immediately forgotten. The veils are put back in place, the doors are closed – and this is not just because the brain cannot handle the data or simply because the substance is wearing off, but seemingly, because there is certain data that is not beneficial for us to retain in our waking state. What becomes very apparent after experiencing these higher states is that there is much we do not need to know in order to live our lives. Thus it becomes startlingly clear that the human experience itself is, in fact, a focused experience of a sort, whereby there is a lot of data that desires to remain beyond our consciousness, in order for us to carry out our earthly tasks.

These perceptions may strike some as being defeatist, but perhaps also imply a kind of learned surrender to higher orders of intelligence. I think the mistake that some people may make with DMT is to try and crack the cosmic code and completely uncover the mysteries. Yet there is no code that needs to be hacked, the code is simply present and can be read by those able to interpret it. As the Indian mystic Ramana Maharshi famously stated, it is all an 'open secret'. It is then a matter of human beings being able to interpret what is actually present, and to then be responsible for the ramifications of that interpretation. To be responsible for states of integrity and unity is to not perpetuate fragmentation, selfishness and immature agendas that do not further gnosis or connected relationship.

It could also be said that there are no mysteries and all is present, but all is mystery because there is so much that is incomprehensibly complex for a single human mind to understand. We don't have to completely understand, and can simply put effort into interpreting what we can. Different interpretations can then be utilised, and in many respects, we are all like the blind man fascinated by the front of the elephant, describing the trunk as if it was the elephant! It is necessary in a survival sense to relay an interpretation of phenomena, which allows us to fight or run away. That is, our ancestors had to understand the mammoth and its most basic behaviour in order to kill it.

Reductionist science reduces a phenomenon to its mechanistic parts in order to understand it enough to relate to it in terms of domination, that is, the ability to predict its behaviour and kill it, if necessary. But the 'reduced' explanation is not the actual thing in itself, and the interior nature of the thing represents much more complexity and meaning; and this interior meaning is what artists often attempt to capture. Regarding the smoked DMT experience, fragments of a reduced explanation will often not do justice to what we experience, and what's more, there is typically very little in our world which high dose DMT experiences can be related to. There is quite clear 'meaningfulness' to a good, solid breakthrough experience with DMT. If the experience does strike one as being meaningless, then it may only represent what Buddhist meditators call the 'lesser lights'. Even stunning geometric patterns and visions of flowers and so on, may be considered lesser lights within that paradigm. ("If you see Buddha on the road, kill him!") There are some beings and forms which show repetitive themes that are quite simple in nature and do not emanate much in a way that truly captivates the attention.

The key to real breakthroughs into the realm of the inexpressible is actually smoking enough DMT. Even experienced smokers have been known to say that they have never broken through with DMT. The smoke is very harsh, and unless someone is there to guide you, it can be quite tricky to smoke enough to have a breakthrough experience. Breakthrough is unmistakable however, as the experience is shocking and immense. As Terence McKenna said, "If you could die by astonishment, you would." However, being able to integrate such experiences can be hard for Western minds who may experience the fantastic and the alien, but not be able to interpret or integrate such experiences effectively into their regular living framework. Many have difficulty in merely acknowledging the vastness of what is revealed, as their paradigms of thinking may be quite limited in comparison to the immensity of what has been experienced.

But what does all this mean? What use is it? If you subscribe to the theory that these visions are just some kind of aberrant hallucination – an artifact of brain functioning – then it cannot mean very much, at best it is all merely imaginal. That these experiences do mean something to almost all people is the anomaly in this case, and this meaning can then have profound consequences for the individual. And what is that? The scientific materialist paradigm predominantly believes in itself recursively, and nothing that it cannot describe or 'prove'. What cannot be described or understood within the constraints of that paradigm is 'paranormal' and must then, in fact, be unreal. What is immaterial – the interior dimensions of human experience, is not normally considered real data within that paradigm, as such data is not measurable or quantifiable and cannot easily be subjected to empirical 'experiments'. Furthermore, this sort of data does not help us hunt the mammoth – that is, it is not of immediate practical benefit for the survival of human beings.

Typical human consciousness is so focused on survival, within the mental dominion of 'hunting the mammoth', that the inner world is not typically easily described in the languages of most cultures. Yet, even in the comparatively emotionally stunted English language, we can communicate something of an inner world, and we have some words that can represent that inner world. Yet, the 'highest' levels of the smoked DMT experience simply cannot be expressed with human language, and you will know when you have truly gotten there – when there are simply no words to describe the sophistication, immensity, and complexity of what you have experienced.

Malevolent Beings and Schizophrenia

Not all the beings you can meet in the psychedelic space are pleasant, and some are downright malevolent. That being said, they do not have the power to kill or maim the physical body. You can even come across malevolent entities in ordinary life. Many years ago, I gave a talk at a venue, only attended by a man who sat right at the front, who I later found out was one of the founding and leading members of a large international cult – one that had its headquarters only a hundred metres from the venue where I gave the talk. Afterwards, I went home with a friend, and we both found ourselves silently engaged in a state of great strain and internal conflict in which we both felt drawn away from our present path for some hours, only able to hang onto the couch and exclaim our baffled confusion.

After some time, the strain and internal conflict passed, and we both wondered what it had been about. We both came to the conclusion it must have been related to the ex-cult leader who had come to my talk and who sat right at the front. A year later, I happened to attend a meeting of the cult in question. What I perceived at the meeting were people who felt they were 'going into the light' via some sort of 'Pentecostal' experience. However, I could see they were actually feeding a large amorphous being with their energy in exchange for some sort of presumed higher experience. Having perceived this in a psychic sense, I went outside the building into the garden and proceeded to talk to this being for about half an hour. I explained to this being that what it was doing with the humans was duplicitous, and that using humans as an energy source was not ultimately satisfying for itself and its own needs. I eventually convinced the being to leave and to find a more satisfactory energy source. I noticed in the following months that the significant power and influence of this cult over the community ceased almost entirely and the centre shut down later that same year. At the time, I could not help but see a correlation between the existence of this being and the very existence of the cult.

I know to most people, this would all appear very far-fetched and could only exist in the realm of the imagination. But whether you consider such malevolent beings imaginary or not, they can appear and do communicate. I would say the most obvious power they try to utilise is that of persuasion. Like school bullies, they will tell you a version of reality which is certain and inflexible. There is often a harsh, jagged, forceful nature to their determinism. They often do presume to try and persuade and determine reality for you, and so it can take a strong mind not to be swept into their version of reality.

In my early explorations, various malevolent beings appeared to me, and I began to make peace with them rather than fight them, living in compassion and engaging in dialogue, melting the barriers between them and myself. At that time, I found this tactic to be very effective in dissolving any power they had over me. Many will say such beings are only projections of the internal psyche. Others will say there is only the 'self' and such beings must be part of myself. That could also be said of the human world – that all the beings you meet are a reflection of yourself, which could also be perceived to be true enough! However, these sorts of simplifications often end up becoming quite hackneyed and useless in the real world for the individual. These malevolent beings are normally quite distinguishable from the benevolent beings that are artists, who are friendly and with whom you feel immediate trust. People in meditation circles also speak of malevolent beings dressing up as benevolent beings to trick and fool humans.

So I noticed the further I went into the depths of the visionary space, the deeper the obstructions and the more powerful and gnarly these beings became. Some were clearly gatekeepers of a sort; and with other beings it was often difficult to really know who or what they were. Some of these beings are not just malevolent, but operate in a way that is misleading and sneaky. But how to regard them? And what to do about them?

Acknowledging the existence of these beings is a tricky matter in Western culture. These are the voices that 'schizophrenics' hear, taunting them and telling them to do bad things. Western psychiatrists do not usually acknowledge there is any validity to this phenomenon, as it is the 'unseen' and therefore unreal. In the West, we propose that those people hearing voices are clearly psychologically ill, because it is perceived that their dysfunctional brain is generating aberrant phenomena. To admit the reality or validity of such phenomena is then also to admit defeat to the apparent unknown. And it is only through psychiatric medication (which typically impairs proper brain functioning) that the voices stop, not through psychotherapy. Of course, these anti-psychotic medications block and disrupt certain functions of the brain, rather than addressing the core issues that bring the phenomena to exist in the first place. Many thinkers, such as maverick Scottish psychiatrist R.D. Laing, have communicated that the schizophrenic experience can indeed be valid, in that schizophrenics may often access states of higher human potential.

Yet, there are many different kinds of mental illness. Some mental illness may, in fact, demonstrate possession of various kinds. In Brazil, the 'Spiritist' cultural movement is followed by 20 percent of the population; and they run dozens of mental hospitals, in which psychiatrists and mediums regularly work together to practice dispossession of malevolent beings. That being said, it is my view that when it comes to working with people not in dire need of help, a psychiatric attitude may often be more conducive than a purely shamanic approach. That means focusing on dealing with the root core of problems facing individuals, rather than primarily dealing with the associated beings and entities drawn to the individual, as they will continue to draw such entities and beings to themselves unless the core issues are dealt with. On a psychological level, most people need their 'demons', and have their demons for a reason. Addressing the demonic level does not address why the person has the demons, and many exorcists and healers will commonly communicate that without addressing possibly multi-faceted core issues, that the symptomatic 'demons' will simply reappear again in different forms.

Psychedelics can bring us to face many deep, internal issues often in a ruthlessly direct way, or in a gentle way, and it can be with the help of psychoactive plants that people can release malevolent forces from within themselves. For most people, it is perhaps more significant to understand that the primary hazard is likely to be inside them already in the form of their own thoughts, emotions and behavioral patterns, which is the root cause of all malignancy.

A Simple Analysis of the Perspectives of Benny Shanon

Benny Shanon is a professor of psychology at the Hebrew University of Jerusalem, best known for his 2002 book *The Antipodes of The Mind: Charting the Phenomenology of the Ayahuasca Experience.*

The following excerpts are from a paper by Benny Shanon called *The Epistemics of Ayahuasca Visions:*

> "There is no question about it, ayahuasca induces personal insights, self understanding, and novel psychological comprehension. First and foremost, these apply to the drinker him/herself. In this respect, ayahuasca sessions may function as dense psycho-therapeutical sessions. After my very first encounter with the brew, I have felt that in a couple of hours, I have learnt more about myself than in several years of psychoanalysis. Attestations of this kind are very common, and the sentiments they convey usually remain long (at times, even very long) after the ayahuasca experience itself."

Many people report a feeling of greater empathy, going beyond the walls of one's skin and a greater intuitive understanding of others and themselves.

"The following example of my own happened during an ayahuasca session held in a hut, in the midst of the Amazonian forest, early in the morning. I was looking at the leaves of plants observing how they were directed towards the rays of the sun. I felt I was actually seeing the nurturing sustenance of the solar light. Have I obtained any 'information' I had not known beforehand? I doubt it. But I was open to see the world in a new light, perhaps in the manner a poet or an artist may."

Shanon clearly sees information as being the most important factor we can encounter in the ayahuasca space. In this case, he is seeing the sun as information. This is perhaps not such a banal observation, as without the sun to feed the plants with their light, life as we know it on earth would not exist.

Certainly knowledge can be powerful, but the fruit of such power is not the be all and end all of human value. Shannon contends that ayahuasca does not offer factual information, and I would agree with him if we only include earthly human knowledge in our definition. Yet, I would contest that such knowledge or information is readily available in the human world and the transfer of such worldly information was never supposed to be the primary meat and meaning of an experience of drinking an ayahuasca brew. Shannon talks of telepathy, and I think an important issue to understand is that telepathy is not just a transfer of information. 'Psi' cards, for example, are an information transmission for the sake of psi research. But the need to communicate real meaning is what typically allows authentic telepathy to occur, and on a personal level these communications are much more expansive than mere factual information.

"Whether or not ayahuasca drinkers can actually discover anything new about the external world, be it physical, biological or social, they certainly encounter novelties in the domain of subjective experience."

This could be perceived as quite an externally focused, left brained and masculine perspective. Again, we talk of values here, as discovery of the 'new', in the 'external' or outer world as being of the most value, when the ayahuasca experience primarily takes us into the internal world. The internal world is, of course, typically viewed as being subjective. However, there may be a point in human internal comprehension that shared understanding transforms what is currently perceived as subjective into a collectively shared comprehension, in a way that presently exceeds our understanding. This shared comprehension may already be the case, for example, when groups of people experience exactly the same thing under the influence of a psychedelic compound.

Those shared experiences of what would normally be considered subjective internal experiences are quite commonly reported among psychedelic users. A friend told me how a small group of his friends on very strong LSD saw a tree turn into millions of little diamonds, fall onto the ground, and then reassemble itself back into the tree. I have also experienced being in a small group of people who, after ingesting an African plant entheogen, experienced pretty much the same internal visual data at the same time as the other people present. In this case, we are no longer talking of internal interpretations, the basis of the subjective, but an objective experience reported internally by all participants.

New information and knowledge appears to represent more power, but with the advent of Google, information is abundantly accessible, whereas, having an experience of plants receiving the sustenance of the sun brings a person back into an experience of nature, of the natural world. How does this type of direct seeing change the way humans look at the world and how may it change their thought processes and the way they operate in the world? We are then talking about receiving or having impressions which are not normally seen as valuable, but do we truly understand what value and meaning are?

Benny Shanon's book *The Antipodes of the Mind* sheds some insight into his views of the internal worlds that ayahuasca opens up for most people.

"If the astral is to be conceived as a realm endowed with some sort of concrete, quasi-physical reality (as contrasted with abstract, ideological status) which is not dependent on the minds of human beings, then I categorically object to it. I do not believe there are physical places other than those in the ordinary natural world, I do not believe there are beings and creatures just like us who reside elsewhere in other realms, I do not believe in reincarnation and paranormal travel."

If we look at the Oxford dictionary's definition of paranormal, it says, 'denoting events or phenomena such a telekinesis or clairvoyance that are beyond the scope of normal scientific understanding'. The 'paranormal' is not considered to be normal, but could the paranormal, in fact, be normal in the depth and expanse of inner space?

The evident bias against the paranormal in academia is firstly an emotional prejudice – a political bias within the realm of intellectual thought that does not like to acknowledge there is much more that is unknown than there is known. Modern day academia is largely not open-minded, but close-minded to phenomena that is not easily contained, understood, or controlled by traditional methodologies or systems of understanding – normally what the backbone of academia actually represents.

Shanon further states:

"I recognize that experientially, under the intoxication people do, indeed, feel that what is seen in the visions are wondrous realms that have an actual, independent existence. I have experienced this firsthand. However, I am a western university professor, a psychologist and a philosopher, not an Amerindian shaman nor an adherent of any Afro-Brazilian cult. Thus, acknowledging the enchanted nature of the ayahuasca experience, I am trying to account for it while at the same time respecting frames of thought and canons of judgment that define my own cultural and professional heritage. Admittedly, not always is this easy."

At the same time, he is in a sense, disrespecting frames of thought and canons of judgment, not just of traditional South Americans, but of modern explorers as well. In the global ayahuasca world, among the people who have drunk ayahuasca over say 100 times, I have only met one other person who believes the ayahuasca visions are not as they appear to be. The view that what ayahuasca reveals, does not have an actual independent existence, completely goes against the grain of all indigenous traditions related to the plants, and normally the very meat and meaning of the experience itself. For indigenous shamans, ingesting psychoactive plants is not a matter of wish fulfillment or fantasy. It is a matter of being practical and it is a completely matter-of- fact experience. The fact that many psychoactive plants are utilised by indigenous shamans for the purpose of divination attests to the pragmatic nature of the visions and information received by these shamans via these plants.

To suggest to the shamans that they are simply deluding themselves into believing that they are communicating with plants is clearly the height of 'younger brother's arrogance. 'Occam's razor' is normally used as a skeptical tool, a doubting tool in the case of the 'paranormal'. In this case, we can turn it around. The simplest answer is not to say that hundreds of thousands of people have been deluding themselves or that modern day ayahuasca drinkers are basically masturbating themselves. The simplest answer is to say the phenomena is as it appears to be. That is, the plants actually do communicate to ayahuasca drinkers, and that the plants do communicate icaros.

For example, when the plant spirit is before you, communicating for many hours, it does not make sense to describe all this as mere fantasy, as wish fulfilment, or as anything else apart from what it is. If that is to be considered paranormal, so what? The word paranormal came long after human beings were having these kinds of experiences. It is quite a head-spin to believe that many thousands of human beings have been fooling themselves for decades learning icaros and communicating with plants – and that they have only been fooling their own mind. Then we enter into quite an arrogant and presumptuous position of completely discounting these people and effectively saying they are stupid for believing in what we say doesn't exist. This tendency only communicates to us the self appointed superior methodologies of the Western intellectual world, which clearly does not like to be challenged to see the limits of its systemised understanding.

It would behoove us to look at this false arrogance of cultural imperialism, typified by that of the missionaries and the anthropologists with their various analytical tools and their lenses, who may actually lack the ability to understand the actual and evident on its own terms. As they look upon the natives as children, it is most likely the natives often look upon them as children – babes in the woods of a much vaster reality. This vaster reality is a reality that is not easily measurable, containable, understood, or mapped out with one theological fell swoop. There is a process of inner work, of deconstructing the mind, of engaging with the truth of the emotions and the subconscious, processing one's obvious issues, purifying the body of accumulated poisons and also understanding the frameworks, limits and insecurities riddling one's cultural lens. Only then does the typically confused and overly headstrong Western mind even begin to truly become sensitive to spiritual realities. The living truth does not conveniently materialise into the domain of innately schizotypal mental maps. Western intellectual culture is based upon certain types of thinking that are quite limited and are so often exclusively founded in the mental domain, so much so that it is normally quite difficult for the individual Western mind to simply give up these maps. However, I think Benny Shanon's last paragraph in his book quite elegantly communicates the evident mystery of the ayahuasca state:

"I can only say that ayahuasca and the philosophical puzzles it raises mystify me now no less than when this brew first presented me with its wonders and struck me with its mysteries. Now, after almost a decade of questing, I am more accepting of this option. Perhaps this appreciation of what I cannot know, what I shall never know, is one of the main lessons I have learnt from ayahuasca. Yet, from a cognitive-psychological point the moral of the story is clear: The antipodes of the mind reveal a geography that is much more amazing, much more wondrous than most, if not all, contemporary cognitive scientists seem to surmise."

I think that if we choose to be invigorated by what we do not know, rather than presuming to know everything, and become excited by the prospect of exploration and discovery, progress can be made. Many otherwise apparently intelligent people mistakenly believe modern science has worked most everything out, which is, of course, completely irrational and even ridiculously stupid. I think this tendency hides a profound ontological insecurity that seems to be the common malady of modern man. At any given time in Western human history, this peculiar sort of arrogance has prevailed, even in the absence of the kind of knowledge that we now take for granted. Psychedelic compounds catalyse elements of the profound and mysterious, which are the norm in these states – and this should be cause for celebration, rather than sour grapes of doubt and skepticism. Here is a new territory that in an ideal world can inspire research, exploration and new knowledge.

Chapter Six

Synthetic Chemicals

Phenethylamines and Tryptamines (or Research Chemicals)

Although the number of synthetic psychedelic research chemicals can seem dazzling, almost all of these chemicals are actually derivatives of either tryptamines or phenethylamines – and significantly, most are phenethylamines. The most common tryptamine found in nature is DMT, and the most common phenethylamine found in nature is mescaline. Alexander Shulgin pioneered the development of synthetic analogues of phenethylamine and tryptamine compounds, carefully analysed in his two books, *Phenethylamines I have Known and Loved* and *Tryptamines I have Known and Loved*. In these books, Shulgin reports how such compounds are made and what effect they have when taken at different doses, with assorted commentary about potentials for their use in a conscious and therapeutic setting.

By understanding the synthetic compounds, we can comprehend the natural compounds, because to a certain degree the synthetic compounds must conform to the rules set forth by the existence of the natural psychedelics. It is useful to keep in mind that the synthetic compounds are also working on the same receptors and are in many respects mimicking the effects of their natural counterparts. I believe the key to understanding these chemicals, is that just as psychoactive plants have a deva, or overarching spirit, these synthetic compounds have one as well. Yet, from where their deva is born, I could not say (just as I cannot say where I am most essentially born from). These compounds have an intelligence which has consistent characteristics, and they seem to have a soul, related to the specific batch of the compound, and also an over-lighting intelligence or oversoul. I call this deva or spirit of the synthetic compounds its 'anima', rather than spirit. Jung used the Greek word anima to describe the feminine aspect of a man's psyche, yet the meaning of the word has no implication of masculine or feminine, and the word literally means 'spirit' or 'soul' in Latin.

Research chemicals may well have their uses, but personally, if given the choice between mescaline from the cactus and 2C-B, I would take the cactus every time. If given the choice between Foxy (5-MeO-DIPT) and a sweet ayahuasca brew, it would be ayahuasca every time. There is a warmth, a glow, a light just not found in the synthetic compounds. Having said this, there have been times in the past, when I felt that the synthetic compounds were the way and the truth, and that was perhaps because they possess none of the innate barriers to the psychic depths that the natural compounds include. I have found out the hard way, a few times, that going beyond those barriers is normally not a good idea. Others may disagree with me, and say we must crack the matrix code veil via any means necessary. But I don't believe that is to be done via ingesting a synthetic compound on some sort of individual vision quest.

I think the matrix code veil is there for a reason and acts as a protective sheath to prevent the dunderheaded humans from going into deep water too quickly – and that deep water can be very deep. It can be problematic to enter into delicate situations that you are unprepared to deal with, and that can cause deep angst and psychic trouble for you and others in ways that may be difficult to truly understand. The first time I ingested DOC at 2.7 mg, I felt that it took me into a state promised by advanced yogic practices, and I experienced a deep realisation of the body's energetic circuitry. I felt connected with myself in a way that the natural compounds did not often seem to allow. This is perhaps where we can seem to find an advantage in the synthetic compounds, because it is as if through their coarseness and disparity from our physicality that we can begin to experience our somatic physicality in counterpoint to their action.

In subsequently increasing the dosage with DOC, I found it gave me much access to a light and a deep space of consciousness in which I felt I was able to release fear and engage more deeply with myself. One balmy summer night, lying in the hammock in the Australian rainforest, I took quite a high dosage of 7 mg of DOC. After it came on, the anima of the compound came to me like an 'OK computer' and told me in a robotic voice that its name was '2,5-dimethoxyamphetamine'.

That night I broke a barrier, trying to grab keys that were swiftly grabbed back from me again. I was possessed with a kind of zest and felt that I was truly breaking through, finding an answer that is needed for the human liberation into hyperspace! At a certain point in the midst of my zeal, a red dragon appeared in front of me, which looked exactly like one of those large Chinese dragons depicted in Chinese mythology. It was angry and looked like it had been given orders to stop me. To cut an embarrassing story short, I ended up on my bed having bad convulsions and engaging in particularly delusionary and silly states of consciousness. Later, I met a few different people who said that this dragon was a recurring part of their DOC experiences as well and I came to understand the dragon was an animalistic expression of DOC anima.

In later journeys with DOC at more regular dosages of 3 - 4 mg, I built a relationship with this compound to the point where it became an ally. Somehow, I was able to open up to this thing, this cyborg, in a way that I was perhaps not even able to open up to with a plant. The nature of the visual information and the lens through which this compound saw the world became evident to me. Much of the domain of this compound that it communicated to me, consisted in how it understood the world via the humans who had ingested it. At that point in 2005, these people were predominantly young American people who couldn't get LSD and were unwittingly ingesting a lot of DOC that had been laid onto blotter and sold as LSD.

Further experiments with DOC had me feeling that its 'fixed' chemical nature was not flexible enough to take me to where I wanted to go. At times I felt it was particularly valuable. While other times, I felt like I was involved in a tardy B grade movie with special effects that only led to more special effects. I also felt the DOC was severely compromising aspects of my being, which often left me feeling very seedy and toxic in the days after taking it.

In contrast, I felt DOI (another long lasting synthetic phenethylamine) to be friendlier, smoother, and much longer lasting. A friend and I took 3mg of DOI on a full moon night once in 2007, as phenethylamines are known to be much more potent taken on a full moon. Under this full moon, everywhere I looked I saw transparent beings that were made of twisting thick tubes made of clear energy. These beings looked like creatures made of bubbles, possessing that same colourful and clear texture of bubbles. When I looked at these creatures they would move toward me and communicate with me. I later realised these creatures must actually be some sort of earth spirits, even though they looked alien.

That full moon night, standing in the middle of a sealed country road, one of these tubular beings came toward me and wrapped itself around me like a bat. Then its mouth became a suction cup. I could actually see the tubes around my body and then feel this being sucking something from my left shoulder, over a period of about 30 seconds. The being then unwrapped itself and dissipated back into the countryside. When I looked down, 'cat's claws' had attached themselves to the waist of my pants. The cat's legs were like ribbons attached to the ground, and around me was a ring of thick and spooky-looking smoke. When I lifted the ribbons up to the moon, they began disintegrating, and the ash fell onto my clothes and hands. After some minutes the ash on my clothes began to disappear as well.

For about a week, I felt my left shoulder was in a lot of pain – not a negative pain, but the pain of readjustment. At the time I understood that this creature had sucked some sort of negativity out of my left shoulder, which then led to a deeper readjustment. Of course, these types of experiences completely change one's understanding of the nature of reality itself. Subsequent ingestions of DOI during a full moon did not bring about another meeting with these spirits, but I did clearly 'see' the intricate functional work of these nature spirits in nature.

Again, the days after these experiences with DOI, I felt quite seedy and disturbed, whereas after taking the natural compounds there will normally only be a pleasant afterglow. The visions, which are what most people go for in psychedelics, are normally never as impressive with the synthetic compounds. I could not tell you of one research chemical that I have found to have a particularly impressive visual characteristics. My one experience with DOI was by far the most impressive visionary experience I have had with a synthetic compound, and I was never able to recreate it.

After taking DOM (a phenethylamine relative of DOC and DOI), the American author Ken Kesey felt it had taken away something from him, something that made him human, and he called it his 'tiller'. I would say that there has been negative fallout in myself and others who have taken these research chemicals. I would not exactly say that these compounds are always malevolent; it is just that they do not innately observe the same rules and regulations that the plants embedded within the natural matrix of the earth do. Their nature is innately cold and psychopathic, and they do not possess the same level of care or concern that natural psychedelics have. And they can also do damage, because as such extremely young 'souls', they do not really know what they are doing. They are trying to do things at times, the same things that the plants are doing, which we would interpret as 'healing' – but their skills as surgeons on the human mechanism in its immense subtlety and complexity is not particularly advanced. The work they can carry out is crude, Frankensteinian, but may at times be strangely effective!

However, my observation is that these synthetic compounds can damage the very complex subtle natural form of the human organism. That is not to say all synthetics will do so every time, but their action upon the body is through a kind of force which can often do some damage – on micro and macro levels. Most of the time, you will feel 'seedy' and a little worse for wear after taking a synthetic psychedelic, whereas after taking a natural psychedelic, you should feel better than you did before taking it, even glowing. The synthetic will often take something away from you, while the natural will add something to you – and this is not news to a lot of people on planet earth who take psychedelics!

It could be argued, that despite all the synthetic compounds that human beings make, nature always does a better job than we can do. Plants have the ability and power to heal through their sentience and advanced ability to proactively affect the human organism and whatever may be ailing us. Synthetic compounds do not possess the same type of aliveness, which enables this kind of sophisticated work to proceed. Synthetic pharmaceutical medicines (apart from antibiotics) never actually cure any condition, while plant formulations traditionally do. It is also worth noting that at least 40 percent of pharmaceutical compounds are based upon plant medicine.

Points of view which state that the only effect a plant can have upon a human is the action of its alkaloids or molecules, are completely missing that there are many subtle communications and interactions which represent the technological communication of the plants. This is why synthetic pharmaceuticals do not have the ability to heal or truly treat a living organism such as a human being, as they are created as mechanical alkaloids having a specific simple action upon the human organism, and that is all! Would you rather have a robot as the ambassador of your country, or a human being who can cajole, charm and understand the intricacies of any given situation?

Utilised for the purpose of self-understanding, however, these synthetic psychedelic compounds can be useful. I can only urge those who want to discover how consciously these kind of compounds can be used, to read Myron Stolaroff's book, *From Thanatos to Eros*, which is available online in its entirety. Unfortunately, the number of people in the world today who use such compounds maturely are very few. The prevailing paradigm of the masses is one of escape and of simply being entertained by the pretty sparkling things, even when it comes to the use of somewhat exotic research chemicals.

It can be exceedingly challenging to use these compounds when you are actually demanding yourself to be present and then working through the deep issues that can come to the surface. This approach differs from the way that, say, LSD was often used in the 1960s, whereby many were taking it to experience higher and more expanded states of consciousness. For sure, various forms of so-called enlightenment can be reached with LSD, yet these experiences are still representative of temporary states. I would certainly never say that taking psychedelics is a way to any state of presumed enlightenment or are some sort of shortcut. Furthermore, as soon as we talk about enlightenment, we are talking about the great golden carrot of the Western spiritual search, which ironically enough, only effectively began in earnest after Westerners began to take LSD in the 1960s.

I believe 'enlightenment' is simply a relic of spiritual materialism, ancient and modern. It is the ego that wants this state of presumed spiritual perfection and the resulting self-importance and status – but at the end of the day, your human state is your human state. We live our lives. There is joy. There is suffering. There is adventure. There is time alone in rooms. We are all asked to make decisions, and we are all challenged with new territory and learnings, whereby we will often make mistakes. What we saw in the 1960s and then in 1970s were people like John Lilly, who tried to stay in the psychedelic state for days, weeks, months, and that approach clearly did not work. For one thing, the collateral damage on the body is just too strong. Secondly, as human beings, we simply just have to deal with the world in its most practical and material sense.

To work with these psychedelic compounds as medicines that resolve one's consciousness and issues is, I think, the most useful and mature way to go about utilising these compounds. The synthetic phenethylamines can be useful for working through what is on one's plate, yet any natural psychedelic can work in the same way. Subsequent to ingestion, one is forced to deal with the truth and actuality of the internal human construct. The ego is confronted and cannot hide. Primary ontological insecurity is brought to bear and everything can be re-examined anew.

The clear standout material for engaging into personal inquiry among the synthetic phenethylamines is called 2C-E, which by all reports, facilitates a most effective state for personal processing. I've taken 2C-E a few times and find it to be like a blank slate, although often quite forceful in its action. On one occasion I took it, its anima appeared to me as a goofy, bespeckled Chinaman with chopsticks, which made sense at the time, as pretty much all of these research chemicals are made in China. The other gem among the phenethylamines is 2C-B. I think that 2C-B can be life enhancing and has as many benefits as MDMA can have in terms of awakening to a vaster appreciation of life. As a substance utilised for sexual healing and work in interpersonal relating, it can also be very effective. Unlike many others, I have never had any luck using 2C-B in a sexual context. The one time I took it and tried to have sex with my partner at the time, it stressed out my system so much that I was not able to maintain an erection, and a powerful pressure just came and went. I felt confused in a way, and then I saw in my visual field a literal 'tearing' occur in real time in the auric fabric in my shoulder. The entire experience then just completely stopped, and I felt collapsed, leaving me in a depleted, seedy and sullen state for the next few hours. For the next few days, I felt extreme sharp pain in the spot where I had seen the tear in my shoulder, with no other apparent cause than what happened when I took the 2C-B. This experience tends to corroborate what smug 'spiritual' people will often say: that psychedelic drugs will put a hole in your aura. Spiritual healers who have done a lot of healing work with me have subsequently asked me, with a quizzical semi-horrified look, exactly what drugs I have taken? So, perhaps much of the damage can be repaired, but perhaps much of it can't be either. It is perhaps a kind of disinformation in the 'new age' that all psychotropic drugs will put holes in your aura. I have never had such experiences with psychoactive plants, and such disinformation may well represent a reticence in 'the new age' – a fear of engaging into the deep truth and awareness these plants can bring. However, I've had many experiences where I have felt and seen deleterious effects upon my aura, subtle energy field, or robotic avatar suit, through the use of synthetic phenethylamines and tryptamines.

This is not to say such potential side effects should stop those who feel they can do deep healing work with such synthetic compounds. I have personally guided people into some of the deepest, most potent spaces of immense transformation with 2C-B and MDMA. These side effects are quite relative as well. At one point in South Africa, it has been reported that the Sangoma shamans there were buying legal 2C-B to do shamanic and divination work because their traditional shamanic plants were said to be expensive, hard to prepare, horrible to ingest, and often gave them very difficult and even deadly physical side effects.

In terms of the classic synthetic tryptamines – 5-MeO-DIPT or Foxy – is a clear standout, in particular for its potential to allow people to reach deeper into their sexuality. However, when working with this compound with two female friends at two different times, both of them found the chemical side effects so deleterious and distracting, they were not able to open up and go deep because of the 'body load' of this compound. With other friends, we generally found that the first time with this compound was the best, the next few times were good too, but then we got less and less out of it. Personally, I've never really gotten much out of the synthetic tryptamines like DPT and AMT, and have always felt they fell far short of a good dose of psilocybin-containing mushrooms.

5-MeO-DMT is another standout synthetic compound. I think vapourising freebase 5-MeO-DMT is by far the best way to take it, and the experience is not just 'DMT without the visuals' as Terence McKenna liked to say. Rather, the experience is quite visceral and often quite pleasurable. I was told by a friend that a man who gave 5-MeO-DMT to ex-crack addicts in London said that they found in this substance what they were looking for in crack! I have participated in sessions in South America, where 5-MeO-DMT was given to people in a group, and I watched them cry and break through, realise things about themselves, and engage into highly transformational spaces. I have also given 5-MeO-DMT to about a dozen people, in a circle, in an urban warehouse, one after the other, with all present finding immense value and meaning in the experience.

With 5-MeO-DMT, the space is highly visceral, and you can feel momentum, a movement of consciousness within, which is often epic in nature. The two batches I had that have been most favourable came from Switzerland. Other batches, presumably from China, were nowhere near as effective or workable. I have also smoked 5-MeO-DMT isolated from *Acacia acuminata* species, and I can say these were my most pleasant experiences. One friend says that smoking 5-MeO-DMT after MDMA is an excellent way to minimise the comedown. It should be said, as stated before, even with compounds said to be 99.8% plus pure, I find there are still often vast differences between batches in terms of their effects.

Some people swear by 5-MeO-DMT. You can reach apparently ultimate states via this compound and there are a few in the world scene who are trumpeting 5-MeO-DMT as the be all and end all of psychedelic illumination! Personally, after smoking and snorting 5-MeO-DMT quite a few dozen times, its synthetic nature grated upon me, and I began to find the states it took me to rather forced and unnecessary. 5-MeO-DMT exerts the same kind of fascination that many have with classic N,N,DMT, simply because of the depth, power, and apparently ultimate states that it can procure. But at the end of the day, one is largely just returning to a primordial, a priori place, and there is not essentially a true furthering of the human endeavour.

I have come to feel that 5-MeO-DMT is related to our sexuality. I have had sexual experiences where the states I am experiencing are very similar to 5-MeO-DMT, which makes me feel that perhaps the body creates this chemical or similar ones in certain states during cosmic sexual intercourse. Perhaps the only release that essentially matters is a sexual release into a convulsive, orgasmic state of essentially natural letting go. Yes, some can reach this place with 5-MeO-DMT, but I am yet unconvinced that 5-MeO-DMT could be considered a primary or exclusively important sacrament. 5-MeO can be captivating, intense, transcendental, and cathartic, and yet the kind of data it presents does not seem to be as valuable or 'life changing' as N,N,DMT. That being said, if I could easily access natural 5-MeO-DMT from plants, I think I would share it with more people, and a lot of them could find great benefit in it. I have limited experience with 5-MeO-DMT extracted from the *Bufo alvarus* toad, but my sense is that for lower doses, around 5mg or so, plant sources seem smoother and more healing.

All the time, new and more novel compounds are being created; but recently, I cannot bring myself to go there, and eating all the letters of the alphabet soup does not seem at all relevant. As I age and become more sensitive, I find the action of these compounds to be too rough and clunky. Besides, the last time I took 2C-P, I continually saw mantis-like beings as if they were associated with the substance itself, using the compound to get into the psychic field of human beings who take such chemicals. I got the same impression when I took a batch of DPT many years ago on a beach near Byron Bay – that I was being observed by cold and sterile beings that were using this batch of the chemical to observe human beings. The experience was not demonic per se, but just too coarse and not worth the heavy body load. Around the same time, I also took winter wood-loving mushrooms (as opposed to 'shit loving' mushrooms such as *Psilocybe cubensis*) that an acquaintance had given me, which had grown around Byron Bay. With their absolute clarity and incredible visuals beyond anything I have taken to this day, and their sweet, smooth, friendly nature and virtually no body load, I think that DPT does not even begin to compare to what a friendly variety of psilocybin-containing mushrooms can provide.

The other well-known synthetic compounds have their virtues and characteristics, but before we get stirred around in the alphabet soup, it is best to stress yet again that these compounds appear to have side effects which are unknown in this day and age. I believe it is very unlikely these compounds will be used hundreds of years from now in a more advanced human civilisation. I don't think they would need to use them, and I believe they would consider the side effects to be a price far too high to pay for the potential benefits of these compounds.

These days nothing 'comes up' when I take synthetic phenethylamines or tryptamines. There are no new thought processes, very little is brought to the surface, and few realisations are going to be had. For people beginning to engage with these materials, that space of self-reflection may be very valuable and worth the potentially very troubling side effects these compounds can have upon us. As a guinea pig myself, I do not feel I have come out a whole lot more worse for wear, but I have so in some ways that are noticeable to myself. So I would encourage others to go to the classic plant entheogens for the safest and biggest bang for their buck experiences. But I also do feel it is useful to be aware of the presence and nature of the synthetic psychedelics, and perhaps not completely discount their possible utilisations.

LSD

Perhaps the primary problem with LSD is that black market LSD can often be incredibly tarnished. Yet, there is rare black market LSD out there made with care, alchemical awareness, and 'love', rather than simply made most economically. In that case, the ergot or lysgeric 'anima' has a smooth journey through the human bio-organism. Although it is often the case that specific batches of the ergot derivative that is LSD do not interface smoothly with the human biology, and can represent an invader rather than an ally that is welcomed into the interactive nature of human biology.

Those who produce black market LSD may often not take the time or money to actually bring through that anima into the product, by cultivating the ergot into a form at which it is optimal, as this takes time, money, and patience. It is the rare chemist who understands that he or she is working with a living process and not just 'dead' molecules that are all the same. The alchemist is one who is involved in these subtle processes, who recognises and is in relationship with the alive nature of what he is working with, treating it with respect and concern in all his actions and momentum, which 'it' will respond to favorably – resulting in a superior product. The process of creating LSD involves quite elementary chemical processes, in which the end result is 'supposed' to be completely the same as other batches and yet, never is the same in the ingestion. Experienced 'trippers' will normally tell you the difference between batches is like chalk and cheese. This is because there is a connection to living natural intelligence in this compound, so LSD is not completely synthetic. As a natural compound that has basically been 'tweaked' into a certain molecular structure, LSD is generally considered to be semi-synthetic.

It appears that on a neurochemical level, LSD mimics serotonin and therefore has access to serotonin receptor sites. At times, it can appear to be that LSD possesses the brain and runs wild. LSD appears to be alive and as such, must be stored correctly and not exposed to unfavourable conditions such as ultraviolet light, or it will begin to die. In his book, *LSD: My Problem Child*, Albert Hofmann, the inventor of LSD, makes it clear that there are no known reasons why LSD creates its intense and vivid psychic effects.

> "The psychic effects of LSD which are produced by such minimal quantities of material, are too meaningful and too multiform to be explained by toxic alterations of brain function. If LSD acted only through a toxic effect on the brain, then LSD

experiences would be entirely psychopathological in meaning, without any psychological or psychiatric interest."

"On the contrary, it is likely that alterations of nerve conductivity and influence on the activity of nerve connections (synapses), which have been experimentally demonstrated, play an important role. This could mean that an influence is being exerted on the extremely complex system of cross-connections and synapses between the many billions of brain cells, the system on which the higher psychic and intellectual functions depend. This would be a promising area to explore in the search for an explanation of LSD's radical efficacy."

The 'influence' in this case, appears to be the ergot sentience, the ghost in the molecular machine of the compound we call LSD. LSD was the primary catalyst of societal upheaval in the late 1960s. Of this there can be no doubt – there would not have been 'hippies' without LSD.

Albert Hofmann further observes:

"A caged community of chimpanzees reacts very sensitively if a member of the tribe has received LSD. Even though no changes appear in this single animal, the whole cage gets in an uproar because the LSD chimpanzee no longer observes the laws of its finely coordinated hierarchic tribal order."

The so-called 'hippie' is the chimp in the cage that no longer recognises the hierarchic tribal order. LSD gave the masses of the West the insight to see that empathetic and emotional human values are true and primary values: not economic, industrial or political values. I suppose the experience of LSD, when one first takes it, is realising the present moment in a very organic and direct manner. One can see the world simply, often with empathy and not through the complexity of the conditioned mind. My perception is that how we see other people on LSD is in some sense how the ergot sees us, as when people first take LSD, many report that human beings can look like crazed monkeys – no doubt an accurate and objective perception!

With friends who are new to psychedelics, I will not say to them that taking LSD is a necessary part of their initiation into psychedelics. Like Albert Hofmann, I would generally recommend taking LSD alone or with close friends, in nature, far away from civilisation. I believe LSD can be a fantastic tool, but it is like all compounds sold on the black market, often not reaching its full potential and often deleterious in nature, as the really pure and well-made material can be exceedingly rare. One way to recognise really good LSD is that you should feel fresher after taking it, and not in the slightest bit seedy or under the weather, but rejuvenated and healed. The best LSD should work like medicine for the mind and the body, and yet, even very well regarded batches will often fall short, due to what seems to be an emphasis upon the synthetic and mechanical nature of the molecule that does not appear to mesh well with the body. The better LSD has an organic and fluid nature, having an ability to mesh and mould and communicate itself to the human organism in a positive sense, whereas more lumpen batches of LSD can appear to displace and disarrange the human body in ways that can be experienced negatively. Even the very best batches of LSD tend to show me images of intricate crashing of micro-machinery in my brain, making it very clear to me that some damage is occurring.

LSD commonly takes people on a revelatory journey of analytical self-understanding. I have had fantastic adventures taking 400 - 500 micrograms of LSD by myself in a house in the country. Then I often simply lie down and enjoy the ride, and the resulting experiences can be clarifying, crazy, confusing, and messy – and yet sometimes transcendent, bringing tears and psychological breakthroughs. I have also found that LSD can be useful for deconstructing the ego and for understanding the nature and the content of one's own psyche in a fresh way.

A profound LSD Experience in The Sinai

When I was in Egypt, in my hotel room in the Sinai, I took two Hofmann tabs containing LSD. Normally when I take LSD, I take at least 400 micrograms or so. In this instance, I heard an inner voice pleading with me to only take two blotters, when I was going to take four. Only later did I find out that this acid was unusually strong at 250 micrograms a blotter!

First, I took half a gram of synthetic mescaline, which did not do a great deal. I was left looking at terrain that was featureless and somewhat sparkly, but totally empty. So after a few hours in the mescaline world, I took the LSD. It came on quite fast, and I was immediately driving with great acceleration towards a destiny, myself and yet, beyond myself, careening through the technosphere for some time with great gravity, acceleration and then deceleration through windows of technology and beingness.

Then, looking into the distance, my mind became fixed on a hypnotic pattern like a rapidly unfolding flower, and I went into a trance. The pattern opened up, and emerging from a kind of vortex came a being who would have been no larger than two foot high and less than half a foot wide. I was absolutely stunned, because I knew that this being was the Egyptian goddess Isis. There was golden light around this primarily pink being that also had strangely defined coloured features, which corresponded to images I had seen of Egyptian gods and goddesses.

Immediately, I knelt before this being, as it commanded incredible respect and it seemed to regard me as a small boy. I put out my hands, spluttering, taking great care to receive the blessings from the moving pink tendrils it was bestowing on me. Then, from its eye, to my third eye, it shot a golden beam of light. I was overwhelmed and stunned for a while – in which time the being unceremoniously left.

In my inner vision, I was then shown many screens simultaneously displaying short movies of incredible things that were happening all around the world on this day. I saw the great adventure of life, and that my experience was somehow weaved into one of these great adventures on this day. This experience left me feeling incredibly fresh, as if newly born and very excited. There was something irreversible about this experience. There is simply no way to deny such an experience, as there is a crisp vividness in these trance states that is simply not at all present in the ordinary state of consciousness.

Ketamine

Most people only know ketamine as a party drug, which enthusiasts snort to get wasted, 'out of it', and possibly, if they manage to snort enough of the sharp powder into their nose, go into the 'k-hole'. However, being so-cial or out on a dance floor is about the worst place to seriously experience ketamine. To really experience ketamine you must inject it into a muscle with a needle, preferably human grade ketamine from a vial. A lot of peo-ple have a problem with this method of administration, but having taken ketamine in every other way it can be taken, I can say intramuscular (IM) injection is by far the best way, resulting in the clearest and most satisfac-tory experiences. But it is not the needle that is the problem with injecting ketamine intramuscularly, it is the potentially extremely addictive nature of this compound when you really experience what it has to offer. Indeed, ketamine could be compared to psychedelic heroin, and so many may want to be wary of its very seductive nature.

D.M. Turner in his book, *The Psychedelic Guide* says:

> "After about two years of once per week ketamine use I even found that I had developed an addiction. Although it was less severe than what I've described above, it took considerable effort to break the cycle of repeatedly using it, even though I was aware of detrimental effects that it was causing. Since that time I've used ketamine only occasionally, but find that I must continually exercise a high degree of willpower to prevent my-self from falling into a pattern of regular use. Amongst those I know who use ketamine, I've seen very few who can use it in a balanced manner if they have access to it."

D.M. Turner eventually died by injecting ketamine in a bathtub and drown-ing! So why not stop right there? My view is that when utilised as serious psychedelic medicine, the effects of ketamine are often unparalleled. For example, the Russian researcher Dr. Evgeny Krupitsky used ketamine with great efficacy to treat alcoholics in Russia. I have also witnessed a house-mate permanently giving up drinking a bottle of red wine a night after only one IM injection of ketamine. In my opinion, ketamine is perhaps the most underrated synthetic psychedelic compound with perhaps the most potential value to humans.

For myself, I have found ketamine to be more recreational than useful, but there is certainly some value in understanding those worlds and the various communications of systems of being; sometimes it is like engaging with the machine code of creation. The effect and states that ketamine can take you to at times can be even more startling than full strength smoked DMT, especially when dealing with human grade ketamine from the vial or the very psychedelic S-isomer ketamine.

Much of what one can experience with ketamine represents a kind of dislocation from the physical, of so many non-physical realities that do not really have too much relevance in the human domain. Yet, ketamine can be used to truly let go, because you can engage into other worlds without fear, comfortably making contact with essential states of an expanded reality.

It is clear to many that ketamine is not particularly healthy or good for the body – but I'd say a big night on the town drinking alcohol is likely to cause more irreversible brain damage than taking ketamine one time. That is not to say that ketamine obviously causes brain damage, but there is a very definite sense that it can exert a negative impact upon the nervous system and other levels of the human body, especially when people re-dose immediately and continually.

I have combined ketamine with phenethylamines like 2C-B and DOI, and to a lesser extent, DOC, and have had many powerful and startling experiences. Yet, nothing ever really came out of them. Eventually when I kept trying to repeat these experiences nothing would happen. I was shown how these synthetic compounds were just able to hold or sustain the level of information in a coherent form within the brain and psyche, so I stopped combining ketamine with phenethylamines.

Perhaps one of the most constructive and powerful ways to take ketamine is with DMT, either smoked DMT or intramuscularly. With this combination, the ketamine really relaxes you, so that you can travel deeply with the DMT. The DMT also seems to slow down its effect to fill the ketamine with more colour and warmth than if you had just used ketamine. When IM'ing DMT and ketamine (either in the same needle or in separate needles), there are three dosage ratios I found that work very well: 50 mg of DMT and 50 mg of ketamine is a balanced ratio, or using 100 mg of ketamine and 30 mg of DMT works very well also, or using 100 mg of DMT and 50 mg of ketamine – which tends to be very powerful and has the advantage of letting you go deeper into the DMT space without any resistance. All of these ratios are highly effective and result in pretty much the same kind of extremely potent experiences. I would say taking 50-60 mg of ketamine is advantageous because there is not the same body load of 100 mg or so of ketamine, and it does not take hours and hours to recover from the anesthetic effect; you can begin to walk and function properly again within an hour of taking the lower doses of ketamine.

Please note, it is not easy to prepare DMT in order to intramuscularly inject it. You need to have clear recrystallized pure DMT, bring down its pH to 7 (neutral) and then filter the DMT solution through a micron filter. Failure to prepare the DMT in this manner before IM injection can result in very unpleasant and potentially very dangerous side effects! My observation regarding the DMT and K combination (I have heard of it being called K and D) is that there is a sense the purity of the DMT space can, in a sense, be contaminated by the ketamine, and this may mean you are unable to travel as far and as deep with this combination as you would with just DMT. In fact, I would say that is a problem with ketamine full stop. I sometimes feel that with ketamine, I am interfering with delicate mechanisms that are being forced to move in particular ways that appear to negatively affect the psychic ecosystem of the environments I am traveling in.

I once had an experience where the ketamine anima told me it could not survive my brain, and it showed me it was like a slow bus navigating a busy 20-lane highway. Then there was a bus crash in my brain causing a big pileup. Angry passengers leapt out of their cars and got very upset at the damage to their cars. I then had a headache for days, and for months my conversations were littered with long pauses and memory lapses. However, this experience resulted from using ketamine crystal dissolved back into water for injection, from which I have had other negative experiences.

During later experiments using liquid human grade ketamine from a vial, I had much more powerful and potent experiences. Ketamine that is dried down to a crystal (human grade) is normally nowhere near as good as the ketamine that comes in a vial. It seems to be either the heat or the process of drying (often in a microwave) that compromises the delicate state and nature of the molecule, and then there are adulterants that are often used to "cut" ketamine as well. But strangely enough, some of the best ketamine I have ever had, with the most smoothness and healing qualities, has come from black market crystal.

The ketamine anima can represent itself as a kind of teacher: a young teacher, a robotic teacher, but a teacher nonetheless. Perhaps the ketamine anima is more like an artist. It once asked me, "Why are you so obsessed with the visual input?" while playing me music, like pop music, of an intricacy beyond that of any that I had ever heard. Another time it showed itself as a kind of clear icy crystal like a central computer. I then asked it what it wanted to show humanity, and it told me "teleportation" and showed human beings floating about a foot above the earth, moving about with great ease. There is something to be said about the way you can move around with ketamine, the kind of out-of-body experiences you can have, but often there is an emptiness there. For me, it is the only recreational psychedelic and one I feel that is best tasted only very occasionally. However, I do recognise the enormous therapeutic potentials of ketamine in treating many serious conditions such as depression and addiction.

MDMA and Love

The drug that is called 'ecstasy' is usually a combination of many different compounds and chemicals. However, the primary compound traditionally used as a basis for ecstasy pills is MDMA. Yet there is a big difference between ecstasy, which often tends to be quite 'rushy' and pure MDMA. Pure MDMA at times doesn't seem to do as much as a hard-hitting pill, and you may often feel like you are walking on clouds, while your whole orientation and relationship to reality is quite radically transformed. A girlfriend of many years and I would sometimes take MDMA and really talk. Perhaps this is one of the most useful ways that MDMA can be utilised, to really talk and connect with other human beings. I have met a lot of people who have completely rewired their relationships to humanity through the use of MDMA.

My attitude toward MDMA really changed when I had an experience with an ex-girlfriend of such opening and love, when neither of us had taken any substance at all, which was beyond anything I had experienced with MDMA or any other drug. Why was it that on that particular night we had this experience? When we tried to recreate this experience and took some MDMA together, all I could feel was relative chemical dissonance, and there was an opacity present that would prevent communion and connection in that space. This leads us to the question, why is there love?

When taking MDMA, it is well known by science that there is a release of oxytocin, said to be the chemical of love and bonding. The subsequent relaxation and letting go of defences and armouring can lead to a heart opening, but doesn't necessarily guarantee it. Love appears as a revelation of self-essence and beingness. It feels good. It feels better than anything! It can be the deepest place we can go to. It is powerful and sometimes can seem to be 'too much'. If it is a central and primary value, why is it not our primary value? Yet, as the 'glue' that holds people together, for example, Jesus apparently did not value this aspect of love saying, "Even sinners love their own." (Luke 6:27-32)

Many people in the world seemingly do not realise the existence of love at all. Some people's definition of love only appears to include it as a kind of benevolent sense of liking something, rather than an essential metaphysical phenomena. I only came to truly regularly experience and understand love in a metaphysical sense, after a dozen deep healing sessions with a spiritual healer trained by the Barbara Ann Brennan school of spiritual healing.

People who have had near death experiences, for example, often realise the most important thing in life is what is commonly called 'love'. This is also what happened in the 1960s, when millions of Western people took high doses of LSD and realised, perhaps, that a career in their father's law firm was not going to fulfill their most essential human or spiritual needs.

The most basic and primary perception many people have in psychedelic states or in near death experiences, is realising the essential meaning of what has been called 'love' in the English language for many centuries, is really the meaning and purpose of beingness itself. Then the fledgling explorer, fresh with this insight, looks at the world with this startlingly essential perception and sees that its machines, buildings, and systems do not value the human, and they do not see love in this hugely complex, explicated mind and its creations.

Such individuals may often see the answer as then being in the simple, in the heart, as the heart is so simple it seems. Yet the heart is not an exclusively separate organ. In fact, there is no essential difference between the heart and the mind, as both are an aspect of the same frequency and intelligence; there is no effective dualism in fact. The presumed neophyte 'hippie' does often try to forsake the mind, that there is no 'love' there. Yet, if you let the heart be the heart, love will not necessarily be the result. Love is not the answer, because to assume the answer is love, does not necessarily result in the existence of love! A more essential answer, perhaps lies in generating and maintaining a way of being and living, in which love can live and thrive.

The heart chakra (centered in the middle of the chest) is perhaps an overstated energy centre in the West, but it is a very relevant and real factor, perhaps understated in some cultures, such as Asian cultures. Asian cultures typically value primary centres in the human body, such as the 'hara' (a primary centre of will in the navel) or organs such as the liver or the kidneys. In Chinese medicine, the heart is traditionally perceived as the 'mad king', and the other organs such as the kidneys or the spleen are perceived as the advisors to the king. The neurobiologist Michael Gershon in his book, *The Second Brain*, has shown us that there are about the same number of neurons in the stomach (100 billion) as there are in the brain. My observation is that connection and relationship primarily has its basis in the sacral and solar plexus chakras, as Barbara Ann Brennan observes in her book, *Light Emerging*. The heart appears more of a transcendental medium, but relationship and human connection seem to be based in the two primary vital centres (the sacral chakra and solar plexus chakra) in a more practical and daily sense.

People talk about an open heart or opening your heart. But is this something you can do with your mind? Can a human being say 'let there be love!' and there is love? Not in my experience. The English philosopher Alan Watts has a couple of relevant quotes regarding love. "Never pretend to a love which you do not actually feel, for love is not ours to command" and "There is no formula for generating the authentic warmth of love."

As much as this sounds obvious, it needs to be said. Love is not some schmaltzy sentimental cook up of left-wing hippies; it is at the heart of the meaning and purpose of life. Love feels good. Nothing else feels as good. This is not just falling in love, but the fellowship of man. The love that parents have for their children, that friends have for each other, moments with people we have just met. In that case, there is transcendence; beyond the body we traverse into the space in between each other. We have then horizontally transcended the body and also the mind. There is a cessation of division between us and there is a good feeling of appreciation and understanding of oneself and the other. This feels good. This feeling is deeper than garden-variety pleasure, and there are more refined qualities of texture and colour in it. There is a quality and appreciation involved. There is momentum. There is an activation of our interior nature. We realise our own essence, the flavour and taste of ourselves and the other. Life rewards us with good feelings and good chemicals when we are in a warm and loving space, and life innately punishes us with bad feelings and bad chemicals when we live in a cold and hateful space. This is nothing more than plain common sense. Taking MDMA can help people let go of their defences and experience the frequency of love, but not guarantee it. Personally, I have never had any love experiences after taking MDMA, but other people have awakened love in me, often when I was least expecting it.

Chapter Seven

The Crisis and the Construct

The Shaman vs God

The word "shaman" originates from the Siberian word šamán (meaning 'to know') and was popularised by the largely theoretical Romanian scholar Mircea Eliade. With the publication of the first of Carlos Castaneda's books, *The Teachings of Don Juan* in 1967, the general public began to access the ideas of practical shamanism. Castaneda's first book was a relatively straightforward anthropological work, yet his many other books venture into territory far outside the scope of any traditional form of anthropologically known 'shamanism'. His work represents to me quite a critical perspective of the Western ideological view of shamanism, and I think, clearly shows the restrictions, existential nihilism, and literal folly involved in following such traditions. As much as Castaneda glamourises the 'magical' world of the shaman, I think he also deconstructs the ultimate usefulness or workability of such a rigid path informed by such strict traditions.

Terence McKenna venerated the archetype of the shaman, yet I personally think this archetype represents an outdated model that is perhaps more relevant to how the old world was organised. The majority of traditional cultures have shamanic traditions, and most appear to utilise plant psychedelics. Yet, it is true to say that many shamans do not use or need to use psychoactive plants. In many cultures, those individuals who have a pre-existing tendency for altered states of consciousness are encouraged to become a shaman and for them, reaching trance states to communicate with spirits is not difficult – through dancing, drumming, or simply sheer intent.

Western people are often quite culturally insecure and will seek other traditions that have an apparent understanding of life's spiritual dimensions, attempting to adopt those traditions as their own. My contention is, and always has been, that transplanting different cultural traditions and viewpoints onto the Western culture does not offer us the richness and fullness of potential within which to work, play, and heal. It seems to me that Westerners are often quite loath to face their cultural insecurity and would rather find solace in a cultural transplant with its religious rules and guidelines to follow. In many cases, Western 'shamans' will draw from many traditions to create a syncretic quasi-religious framework. I am not saying that we cannot learn from traditional cultures, but in blindly following traditional pathways and their particular rules and limitations, our naturally creative 'presentness' is often lost. The traditional form of the ritual is like a rote, a magic formula, a technology, but it is not presently creative and requiring aware interaction. Therein lies the present sense of humanity and the present moment of beingness – and it is also true to say that much of the true essence of authentic shamanism requires spontaneity, ingenuity, and present moment problem solving in the realm of the metaphysical, the physical domain and their intersection.

I have seen many in the West attribute miraculous powers they have read about in books like Carlos Castaneda's to indigenous shamanic figures. That is not to say that indigenous shamans do not have the power to heal, as that is the first ability of the shaman that is useful to the community. Sometimes it seems that the Westerner wants to possess a 'magical' power simply for the sake of power alone. It is worth nothing, that in the predominant Western religion, Christianity, a person cannot officially be a saint unless they perform miracles. Yet out of the 34 miracles that Jesus reported to perform in the New Testament, 22 are miracles of healing. In the Far East, it is traditionally viewed that any demonstration of 'siddhis' (magical powers), and especially public demonstrations of them, is considered to be very poor form among saints. Jesus seems to be of this mindset when he was asked, "Teacher, we wish to see a sign from you," to which he replies, "An evil and unfaithful generation seeks a sign but no sign will be given it except the sign of Jonah, the prophet." (Matthew 12: 38-40)

There is something incredibly potent in being able to manipulate 'nature' with the human form that cannot easily be discounted. A man or woman empowered to transform nature is one who is then no longer in battle with it. Have one fish and you can have 200 fish. Your 'magical technology' has then won over nature, in the same way 'science' appears to have won over nature, so perhaps the allure of magical power has the same appeal that science has for many human beings.

It is indeed plausible that Jesus ingested Syrian rue and acacia for their profound psychoactive effects not dissimilar to Ayahuasca, as both plants commonly grow in modern day Israel. And it is not at all far-fetched that Jesus could have been initiated by the Essenes with the psychoactive plant alchemy of the Syrian rue and Acacia. The Israeli psychology professor Benny Shanon believes that Moses may well have been intoxicated by the DMT-containing smoke of the burning bush, which was probably an acacia, as there is largely no other vegetation in the Sinai but acacias. If these theories are at all accurate, the true nature of the Judeo-Christian cultural and mystical roots may well lie in the plants or in the mystical states offered by such plants.

It is probably impossible to offer proof regarding these matters, as we are dealing with events that occurred more than two thousand years ago. If there is proof, it may be within the extremely secretive Vatican library, known to contain a very large number of ancient manuscripts not accessible to the public. This might sound fantastic to some, but let us not forget that one of the most primary Masonic symbols is that of the acacia, a tree that is not native to Europe. Perhaps the acacia represents some secret knowledge brought back from the Middle East by the crusaders, specifically the monastic order of the Knights Templars. The Knights Templars were in the end tortured and killed by the church, as a threat to ecclesiastic power. Let us also not forget that it is commonly observed that many Knights

Templars fled to Scotland and set up the Scottish Rite of Freemasonry. It is also a fact that Rick Strassman's research into DMT was largely funded by the Scottish Rite of Freemasonry Schizophrenia Research Program, as reported on page 113 in his well-known book, *DMT: The Spirit Molecule*.

With psychoactive plants we can have direct access to the spiritual worlds. Then we do not even need the shamans or priests to tell us how it is, because then we can see for ourselves, and learn for ourselves. Then we are not controlled by the primitive men who believe that power lies in control, because what will we do if we are not controlled? Many modern day human beings do not have the commitment to face the inner world, to do the work and pay the price for whatever collateral damage there may be, if indeed there is any at all. Yet quite easily, countries and thousands upon thousands of men will go to war and pay the ultimate price in collateral damage for many worldly and much lesser agendas. At the end of the day, what damage does there lie in ingesting these plants and letting go into what actually is? There is none, but only the potential to be exposed to a vast personal and transpersonal truth that men and women commonly fear beneath their psychological armouring and shielding, and that is a raw reality which innately requires heartfelt consideration, profound inner work and subsequent outer change.

My contention is that these teacher plants are simply teacher plants, helpers, tools, catalysts – but not the Holy Grail. I believe that many of us can become too enraptured by these plants and what they offer us. Many are enchanted by the lesser or greater lights on the cosmic super highway. My perception is that within our bodies we can reach states much more 'natural' and useful to us. Through relationship, love, and sexuality, our primary communication to each other becomes apparent, and psychoactive plants can only accentuate those potentials.

Religion gives human beings an excuse to share the same beliefs, act in the same way, sing the same songs, and dance the same dance. But is that dance one that emanates from within us? Or is it a prescription that we must follow? Personally, I think that creativity is not just a faculty that artists must cultivate, but also a practice necessary for individual health. Many religious traditions preclude creativity, because by following the ritual, we are completely enmeshing ourselves within an inflexible structure or format. That is not to say the format or structure is worthless, but I think it is clear that by strictly maintaining an inflexible structure, we can lose our unique, natural and organic way. Or did we ever even develop it?

Much of Christian theology contends that Jesus, in his divinity, is separate from man, and therefore that God must be separate from man. With tryptamines, the first realisation many have (and for many it is a continuing realisation), is that 'God' is not separate from man! The individual realises 'I am that', a term that can be said in Sanskrit in many different ways, including 'that thou art' or 'I am that I am'. The meaning of these terms is to communicate an ultimate reality, which is that which permeates all, which nothing transcends, and which like the universal space around us fills everything completely from within and without, as the supreme non-dual Brahman. These understandings clearly challenge the comparatively unsophisticated Middle Eastern monotheistic religions that historically place God and man apart.

The 'Easterners' very clearly have had a much more sophisticated spiritual understanding than we have found in the West. Easterners have not argued about petty issues of theology for hundreds of years as Westerners have, but have addressed deeper metaphysical issues in languages such as Sanskrit, over many thousands of years, in a far more adept way than any of the Romanised languages of the West. In the East, advanced metaphysical practices have traditionally prevailed, and to some degree, we can find such practices in the Middle East as well. Westerners are heathens in comparison, as European tribal peoples were ripped from their pagan and natural connection with the earth by the Romans and their church, and plunged into the dark ages for 1000 years, during which time the Western mind was heavily constrained and repressed by Christianity.

The Manual of Western Spirituality

I strongly subscribe to what Jiddu Krishnamurti spoke of, namely that 'truth is a pathless land'. That all human-created structures of religion are not truth, that all their paths to truth and their versions of 'truth' are simply human fingers pointing at the moon that cannot in themselves be truth. All these religious ideas appear to represent a sense of power that an opaque series of thoughts has. True vulnerability and openness to relate, to be present, lies in not holding ideologies of intent, action, and thought, as this is not being present in the intricacies of the moment – this is being elsewhere, seduced into a false power, which gives off the glamour of illusionary 'otherness' or 'somethingness'. In many cultures, a lot of apparent tribal credibility appears to be based on possessing the mystique of these forms of 'power'. Often it seems that these structures of power are attempting to mimic the internal power, the internal intelligence which is present, which is not 'other'. It is here now. To truly utilise the human intelligence can be quite a challenge. It requires practice and you may make mistakes, but following the well-worn track only brings stagnation and the same old results, if even that. It could even be said that one of our primary purposes as human beings is to develop our natural and innate human intelligence. Therefore, formulaic religious forms of thought could be perceived to be inhibitive to human evolution.

By ingesting the plants we are essentially called to an ontological nakedness, a natural and organic place where we must call on our devices and abilities in the present to navigate and work out our present orientation and process. This is shamanism and it is also not shamanism, as the idea of shamanism can give us the idea that self-navigation is a special thing. By continually referencing the manual, we are not living, as the manual is not life. The manual is someone's interpretation of how we should proceed with our actions. Underlying a very common reticence to operate from natural intelligence, there often appears to be the fear that we are bad, that by not following the 'good book', we will do bad things. I think many realise that a true and innate ethical and empathetic framework exists within and without us, and this is how it is possible that human beings can naturally truly grow and evolve.

In being overtly controlled by systems of thought, we do not authentically learn to be ourselves. We then do not comprehend our animal nature and how to befriend, evolve and transform what it is. Instead, we try to control and tie up our inner animal. Is our commitment to life or to procedure? Collectively, is our priority to life or our ideologies of want, some sort of illusion of smooth sailing that systemisation supposedly brings? Yet, how is real meaning in our lives created? I suppose that the majority in the world today would say the most real meaning they experience is through their relationships – family and friends. The medium that allows our relationships (say 'money' or 'religions') represents intermediaries that often create division and war – the antithesis of relationships. The fruit of our relationships, love and fellowship, are seen by many to be the highest priorities in human life. Could there be another priority more esteemed than that? Perhaps this imperative could be perceived as a kind of self-development that allows personal and interpersonal virtue and maturity, the learning of how to truly and effectively be with ourselves and each other.

Religions do bring people together, but so does music, so does art, so do shared interests, like sport. The drinking of ayahuasca brings people together as well. People often tend to be quite attached to how they drink ayahuasca, what shaman they 'use', how he works or doesn't work – and to be quite serious and earnest about it. The drinking of ayahuasca can become quite religious for many, with its different cliques, sects, and theologies. Without any of these structures, we are all left with each other and are brought to each other, and are yet still ourselves. Perhaps the collective and communal nature of the ayahuasca experience is overstated or exaggerated. If the dose is fairly strong in terms of its DMT and beta-carboline content, movement will not really be possible, and one will not even be aware of one's surroundings, and there will be only immersion into what is present.

The attempt to get off the wheel via the religious enterprise and the certainty of its prescriptions and perceptions seems ludicrous at times. Religion itself may often represent a greater obstacle to a living, direct realisation than it claims to be. In the Judeo-Christian perspective, we are not even supposed to take this life seriously, and to 'hate' it: "If any man come to me, and hate not his father and mother and wife and children and brethren and sisters, yea, and his own life also, he cannot be my disciple." (Luke 14:26:) Perhaps, that is because religions typically claim to offer something more than 'worldly' life.

But does 'otherworldly' life make any sense while we are having a human experience? When we begin to go out of the body, one realises the domain of possible experience is much, much larger outside of this apparent physical framework. But at the same time it is the present physical framework that we are faced with, its challenges and nature that we must deal with, individually and also collectively. Many spiritual traditions promote the transcending of this reality, or deny its validity. In beginning to travel outside of the realm of usual human awareness, it would initially appear that these realities are much more interesting than ostensibly mundane activities, such as mowing the lawn or cooking spaghetti. However, when we learn the value of this human experience, we can see our own potentialities and find solace, fulfilment and redemption in human life itself. Nothing I am communicating here constitutes a unique or new perspective. Such perspectives have been reiterated by many, especially those who have explored psychedelics, such as the comedian Bill Hicks, who famously said:

> "The world is like a ride at an amusement park. It goes up and down and round and round. It has thrills and chills and it's very brightly coloured and it's very loud and it's fun, for a while. Some people have been on the ride for a long time, and they begin to question: is this real, or is this just a ride? And other people have remembered, and they come back to us, they say, 'Hey, don't worry, don't be afraid, ever, because, this is just a ride...'"

Pitfalls along the Way

What are the negative aspects of the 'psychedelic path'? Well, first of all, taking psychedelics at any sort of decent dose can result in a difficult experience. It is not always easy to face yourself. To reveal the raw truth about yourself, and release the identity of the ego and mind, you must face many fears and be prepared to change, be prepared to die, be prepared to face the unknown and be prepared for a challenging journey. The most negative aspect of psychedelics, in that sense, is that many people choose to give into their fear and not actually take high enough doses to facilitate transformation and authentic healing.

Another negative aspect is the disease of delusion, which often seems to be an inherent part of taking psychedelics, as it is not uncommon to see things that are not actually there and believe things to be true, that are not actually true, when heavily influenced by certain compounds. There are many definitions of delusion, but perhaps the most primary form of delusion is our own realisation of what is actually not true or correct or 'real'. I am not talking about what society regards as real, or what rationality or any system of apprehension of reality considers real, but rather what actually is real for an individual in a practical sense. For example, you could become convinced that your friend Joe wears a wig. When you actually see Joe next, you pull at his hair, and it turns out that it is actually his hair. So you have been deluded to think that Joe wears a wig when, in fact, it is clear that he does not wear a wig.

It is also that many psychoactive plants can straight out lie to people and tell them stories about the future and how reality is or is not going to be. I would say that these plants can often be tricksters, and so it is wise to take what they say with a grain of salt and be wary of any absolute or concrete view of reality they may present. Both myself and many other people I know have been led down the garden path by the plants, forgetting they can be playful tricksters who have a tendency to want to show us our own egoic delusions of certainty!

Some would consider that seeing an aura around another human being is a delusion. But the point is, who can disprove that auras exist? At best, you can say that Western culture and its most esteemed methods have not come to a consensus on auras. However, it is possible to have a photograph of your aura taken, and in Russian science, the aura is often measured with a Kirlian camera. For many people, 'the aura' is an idea that is tied into belief systems and identity. Auras are considered very 'new age'. So seeing an aura may be the start of a slippery slope that will begin with a mild crystal fetish and perhaps end in joining a group of earnest naked men jerking off together in the wilderness. Even though this seems silly, it truly seems to be a fear that certain actions beget a certain identity. A lot of phenomena outside established practice is considered new age, which in turn is typically considered fluffy and soft and is not often taken seriously by self-pro-claimed hard and rigorous thinkers.

Mainstream thinking in the West has historically been quite myopic, in that, throughout Western historical thinking it is assumed that we almost completely know 'what is going on'. When we don't know, it is often that we fill in the gaps with what we do know. Sometimes it seems that only the most mature practitioners of Western intellectual thinking readily accept ignorance or lack of knowledge. We often don't want to acknowledge how limited our data is and how much we don't know, as this makes us feel insecure and lacking the necessary data to 'hunt the mammoth'.

Western history of the past few hundred years represents a continual evo-lution in how we understand the world. As we have gazed into the stars and into the microscope, our understanding of the world has continually expanded and evolved. We are able to see the universe is bigger, more fantastic and sophisticated than we have been able to imagine previously. Yet, at any given time, there are those who maintain that the very limited present-day models are actual truth rather than simply limited models created by a species at a particular point in its evolution and understanding.

Some will say the experiencing of 'supernatural' beings must be delusion-ary. Yet in and of themselves those experiences cannot be delusionary until we can completely disprove supernatural beings, which has not been done. Only the skeptics, those who are philosophically inclined to doubt every-thing not described by the territory of the known map, are curiously prone to certainty of mind that such beings must not exist. Yet the mainstream Western paradigm of 2015, which typically only acknowledges the physical world as real and the non-physical world as a delusion, will eventually ap-pear as a footnote in history. Many will often defend their present version of reality as the indisputable 'truth', and this kind of certainty can itself be perceived to represent a kind of delusion.

A key component of the DMT experience for many is realising that the human mind cannot contain or truly know the immensity of how life works. As radio show host Joe Rogan once said, we are then like a dog, interpreting the human world – you can see what is happening but you cannot understand it, and you know you never will because you are a dog and not a human. What can be experienced with DMT is just so far beyond any of our known paradigms. Within these expansive perceptions is inherent hope, as our paradigm typically positions itself as the only paradigm. Through experiences with DMT, we can realise that we are not alone, not only in the sense of physical aloneness – that we have physical extra-terrestrial brothers and sisters – but that we are not alone 'cosmically' which is, perhaps, even more significant.

Religious cosmologies, similar to all creation stories, tend to have a rather limited scope of understanding the world and cannot normally look past heaven and hell, nirvana, an ultimate creator, or various gods or goddesses. By smoking DMT, you can encounter the completely alien which nothing has prepared you for, and perhaps you will never recover. A lot of people do not seek to go back too quickly. Yet, to see the alien, the 'other', the 'intra-terrestrial' as part of yourself, I think is quite inspirational.

Another aspect of the psychedelic path that many fear, is engaging in a reality that could appear to innately ostracise you from a larger part of the population. Having gone very far and deep, I can say there is a point at which you are free to relate to anyone without necessarily creating contention or conflict with those who may not agree with your perceptions of reality.

Another downside of psychedelics is the potential to become too reliant on the compounds and plants themselves to experience a state of transcendence or juicy experiences. I believe that when used wisely to work through issues and what is on one's plate, then fulilment and a healthier and more functional state of awareness will result - so that the individual then is more happy in themselves and ceases to want to transcend their own boundaries.

Another possibly negative aspect is the legal side – psychedelics are illegal and they can be hard to obtain, at least in good quality. However, in countries like Australia and most of Europe, simple possession will not land you in jail. It is worth nothing that the only reason that psychedelics are illegal is because LSD caused some social upheaval in 1960's America and one guy jumped off a roof and died. Then in 1971 there was The United Nations Psychotropic convention which pretty much all member states signed as a matter of course, illegalising any of the psychoactive substance which were known at that time.

Flashbacks are certainly overstated and overrated. They are known to occur, but I can't say I know of anyone who has ever had a flashback or thought them to be a real issue. One of the primary issues with psychedelics is ego death, and the time and energy that is necessary to truly engage with the process. D.M. Turner in his classic book *The Essential Psychedelic Guide*, had this to say about dealing with ego death:

> "Psychedelics are much more than recreational drugs. They have the ability to make significant changes in us with a single use. Many advanced users consider this ability to 're-imprint the mind' as the most important benefit of psychedelics. If examined closely, most psychedelic experiences will fit the following model. Psychedelics will dissolve one's identity and perceptual framework, a process commonly called 'ego death'. Next one experiences the raw or undifferentiated energies flowing through their senses from a formless or undefined state. They can tap into the vast banks of imagery within their mind, adding their creative powers to generate limitless visions of intricacy, beauty and meaning. During this time one may try on various 'filters' through which everything is perceived, and create hallucinations or experience many personalities. The journeyer will be outside of their normal conceptual frame-work and will be able to look at their thought processes and personality from new angles. Later in the experience they will re-assemble a new personality, based on their old personality, but hopefully improved.

> In some cases it takes users numerous sessions to go through the process of ego death, and detach from their familiar mode of perceiving things. This often occurs when someone begins

experimenting with small doses, and very gradually increases the amount they consume. In these cases the psychedelic never fully transports them out of routine awareness. When ego death is spread over weeks or months, it can take on strange manifestations as one experiences separation from various aspects of their familiar reality tunnel."

The disadvantage of such an endeavour, according to many, is the shift away from consensus reality, away from the predominantly mainstream society. Many who begin to take psychedelics may find that their own personal shifts necessitate a change in circumstances, whether that is work or friends or so on. But this is life – people change and psychedelics are catalysts of change in people. It is hard to learn life lessons as a hermit in the wilderness, as such learning normally seems to apply to conduct, action and personal character – qualities which are only understood or witnessed in relationship with others. The kind of yogic spirituality that usually only considers the energetic nature of the biophysical self, which is esteemed within some Asian cultures as the highest path, is most typically engaged with after largely completing a worldly life as a 'householder', which means having a job and raising a family.

Another pitfall of engaging deeply with these psychedelic states is that a kind of very seductive inflationary egotism may be brought to the fore. This inflation typically occurs, because as individuals become more and more vulnerable and sensitive, they seemingly need to 'puff' themselves up and put themselves higher on a pedestal as a means to protect themselves. I suppose this mechanism is very similar to how different animals 'puff' themselves up, but in the human sense, it comes in the form of appearing bigger, greater, more 'spiritual', higher, and on a larger pedestal than others. It is true many want to believe in this pedestal or psychic positionality (enlightenment or what have you) to give their power away to presumed spiritual authorities, or project a stage of growth such as 'enlightenment' they too can attain, or even to project their father or mother issues onto such individuals. These tendencies are all too common in the guru/cult leader/religious authority game.

For some strange reason, many people believe that assuming they are actually 'the messiah' gives them an air of invulnerability or ultimate power. Yet, they might want to remember what was done to Jesus, or the Sufi mystic Hallaj who proclaimed "I Am Truth" and for which he was cut into pieces, among many others in history who have openly proclaimed an exclusive or special divine nature. Any individual is clearly mistaken to think he is Jesus, as nobody can ever be the historical Jesus again. Many would say that ultimately, you are Jesus in the sense that all are the Christ. Being the best you that you can possibly be is the only thing you can do – Jesus had a life, and you have a life. What are you going to do with it? Jesus said, "By their fruits, ye shall know them", so what are your fruits? I'd say a kind of messianic zeal can be quite common for people who engage in truly pursuing the psychedelic path and can represent a kind of stage or test. I guess if you fail the test you start wearing flowing robes, wear your long hair with a beard and become an ineffectual Jesus wannabe! Pass the test, and perhaps you can really become and embody yourself, and start giving some valid value to the world, reaping the fruits of the many seeds you sow, and becoming an authentic human being in a profound state of learning and development, who can connect to others and the world around them. People who become possessed by their ego, who want to believe in a final state of rest or perfection such as 'enlightenment' or 'messiahship' are sadly all too common.

This essential truth of this presumed messianic consciousness, which is a collective consciousness realised in the human form, can be known as the 'Christ consciousness'. Yet in the teachings of the church, only the Christ can attain that state because he is divine, and we are merely human. Yet, this goes against his very teachings, such as "greater miracles than this you shall do." My namesake, Julian Palmer, was burned at the stake in 17th century England for not believing in the virgin birth. If Jesus was born to a virgin, then clearly he must be divine, (also positing sexual relationship as undivine!) To claim there was no virgin birth then, is to cast doubt on Jesus's divinity and therefore our comparatively undivine nature.

However, the basic point is that this universal and ultimately non-dual nature is not unique to Christ; it belongs to all who can access it and yet it is not always easy to access. With psychedelics, these states can be accessed, and it is possible to experience the interconnectedness of existence and essentially the oneness of all reality. I had a profound experience of being interconnected in the human form, when I first took the synthetic phenethylamine DOB, a substance I do not necessarily recommend taking because of its vasoconstrictive properties, and also my fingers smelt like DOB for six months after taking it. My awareness seemed to extend far beyond my own, over the Earth, for hundreds of kilometres around me, which was a very raw and intense experience. I was instinctively led to a book by Sawan Singh, a teacher of Shabd yoga, and opened to the page where he states: "Many desire enlightenment, but few, if any, are willing to pay the price." I understood that price was letting go of the ego and ceasing to be identified with the ego and body, and more with an a priori identity with this universe, the earth, and all of humanity.

Mystics have often talked of being sensitive to the pain and suffering around them in the human world. Transcendence does not always mean a kind of vertical transcendence, but also becoming and fully experiencing yourself as your surroundings – as many saints and mystics have reported. Christopher Isherwood reports of these sorts of experiences in his book about Ramakrishna, the late 19th century Indian saint:

> "In his transcendental states, Sri Ramakrishna used to feel identified with both living and non-living things. Once near Kali Temple the garden was covered with newly grown grass in the lawn. Sri Ramakrishna in his ecstatic mood ('bhava') transcended the normal consciousness and was feeling identified with the grass when a man happened to walk across that spot. At this, Sri Ramakrishna felt very restless, feeling unbearable pain in the chest, as if trampled by the person walking over the lawn. At another time, on the bank of Ganges, two boatmen happened to quarrel among themselves. Soon a fight ensued between them. Sri Ramakrishna became identified with the weaker of them, and the marks of injury were visible on his (Sri Ramakrishna's) body when the stronger one hit the weaker one. Such innumerable examples can be quoted from his life."

Another possibly negative aspect of psychedelic use is that people can enter into a state that can be diagnosed as hallucinogen persisting perception disorder (HPPD). In this condition, people continue to live in a psyche-delic state of awareness for quite some time after taking the substance. It can be hard to live in a reality where your thoughts become manifest in front of you as soon as you think them. Our society is simply not set up to support the experience of these states in people. This hyper-reality is a kind of awakened state, commonly experienced by those who may call it 'kundalini awakening' or some sort of 'spiritual emergence'. The symptoms of a spiritual emergence can mimic a psychotic and/or manic episode, except lasting over many months. It is then really a matter of coming to terms with the new data, accepting the new data and committing to facing and dealing with it. In addition to finding as much support as possible, it is important in this state to focus on grounding activities such as massage, yoga, exercise, and healthy diet. Often times, what is called HPPD is often only a state of accelerated learning, integration and processing. And after a certain amount of time, even up to six months, the process will normally and naturally conclude. I have experienced staying in a profound expanded state of awareness for a week or two after taking LSD or Ayahuasca, and have found the best way to deal with that state was to choose to engage with the data and process what was coming up until there was a natural conclusion back into baseline consciousness.

For those who have experienced a hyper-real reality, it is not necessarily a preferable way to live. 'Normal' reality, with its slowed down pace involving tea and scones and big novels, can often be preferable to a hyper-reality of alternate dimensions, talking grasshoppers, seeing people's auras, and hearing their thoughts. I once knew a woman who took LSD every week for ten years in her 20's until she began seeing people's auras, which is when LSD ceased to be fun for her. With such power comes responsibility, yet psychedelics can often present a power that many are resistant to fully accept or embrace in all its implications.

Chapter Eight

Working with It

The Benefits of Pure Awareness

When I first encountered the psychedelic world in the late 1990s, I considered it to be a somewhat immature and ill-defined 'path'. My limited experience of the culture led me to believe it was all about the pursuit of tacky psychedelic visions and experiences for its own sake, which seemed cheap and futile to me. My own reading and inspiration at that time lay in those who bridged Eastern mysticism with Western mysticism: writers such as Franklin Jones (Adi Da), Robert A. Monroe, Nisargadatta Maharaj, Alan Watts, Jiddu Krishnamurti and Chögyam Trungpa. I believed these individuals were proposing a serious investigation into the self and the metaphysical nature of human existence. Terence McKenna's thinking did not attract me at the time. I thought his time wave zero mathematics, views regarding DMT machine elves, and exhortations about 2012, represented little in the way of meaty metaphysical content and seemed to me to denote a shallow avoidance of the real and practical nature of human life. However, I later came to realise the incomparable brilliance of Terence McKenna through listening to his numerous talks. Even though 1990's psychedelic culture did not appeal to me, actually taking large doses of psychedelics I found to be startlingly awakening and I started to learn how to utilise these profound spiritual tools.

Perhaps the first stage to realising any sort of authentic spirituality is to realise that there is another reality, an internal reality or internal self, beyond the body or mind or physical world. In the West this 'otherness' has typically been called the soul or the spirit. In many forms of spirituality, realisation of 'the self' beyond the ego is perceived to be enough, and some sort of enlightenment is often promised to those who abide deeply enough in the self. And yet, I never saw this deeper self as an answer in and of itself. For me, I saw that psychedelics naturally revealed impediments that prevented the light or intelligence of the self from manifesting into human reality.

Many Buddhists believe in cleaning the mirror to allow the true light of the self to shine through. *The Diamond Sutra and the Sutra of Hui Neng* from the fifth century AD China communicates this metaphor:

> "One day the Fifth Patriarch told his monks to express their wisdom in a poem. Whoever had true realisation of his original nature (Buddha nature) would be ordained the Sixth Patriarch. The head monk, Shen Hsiu, was the most learned, and wrote the following:
>
> The body is the bodhi tree,
>
> The mind is like a clear mirror.
>
> At all times we must strive to polish it,
>
> And must not let the dust collect.
>
> The poem was praised, but the Fifth Patriarch knew that Shen Hsiu had not yet found his original nature. On the other hand, Hui Neng couldn't even write, so someone had to write down his poem, which read:
>
> Bodhi originally has no tree,
>
> The mirror(-like mind) has no stand.
>
> Buddha-nature (emptiness/oneness) is always clean and pure;
>
> Where is there room for dust (to alight)?"

Buddhists often emphasise the original purity of the mirror and the original nature of all existence as emptiness and oneness. As 'enlightened' as this perspective may well be, it is then also possible to forget to see what is actually on our plate and in a practical human sense; it is also wise to 'strive to polish the mirror and not let the dust collect'. I think it is clear that the beginnings of a mature approach to inner work lies in cleaning the mirror so that the light of self can shine through into awareness. Yet, I do not think that such purification is enough. To truly live the light of the self, we also need to be proactive about how our soul is becoming and being in the world.

The mirror cannot always be completely cleaned through passive meditation alone. When an individual feels stuck or wants to really see what is obstructing him/her on whatever level, psychedelics can really stir the pot and bring unconscious and subconscious issues to awareness. Many people carrying out deep 'inner work' talk of peeling the onion to reveal the inner layers of self. Psychedelics can allow individuals to look at their raw data and work it out within themselves, in a space in which perceptual opt-outs are then no longer as possible. Stan Grof famously said that,

> "LSD appeared to be a powerful catalyst of the mental processes activating unconscious material from various deep levels of the personality."

The role of a psychoanalyst is to help tease out and bring the unconscious material to consciousness, so that it can be processed, understood, and worked out through present intelligence and awareness.

To take a psychedelic compound for self-investigation can include fun, but taking the compound just for fun typically does not include self-investigation. The mindset can be adjusted, developed, and made more flexible – this is the 'set' (mindset) in the two factors of 'set and setting.' One's results are normally going to be related to the mindset and intention that you have. People often smoke DMT or drink ayahuasca because they want to resolve an inner conflict and come to some resolution, or gain some guidance. Not always is everything put on a plate for them, but at the very least, the inquiry is normally pushed forward through to greater clarity and perspective.

Some psychedelics can be used to process intricate, complex material about how you relate to others, how you relate to 'the world', or how different aspects of your self relate to each other. Once this process is started, or you have quite a number of hours in such processes, then psychedelics may become less necessary. After many hundreds of hours of such work, it is very rare for me to really feel I am able to do as much work as I used to when I first started out. Give me 500 micrograms of LSD and my inner world does not vary too much from my ordinary state, whereas most people, even those who are quite experienced, will often experience themselves becoming aware of a lot of dust on their mirror when taking this much LSD.

Many times in the psychedelic state we are confronted by the nature of inter-human communication, especially the roles of masks, identities, human drives, ethics and social expectation. We are then looking in a horizontal plane at what prevents our natural and non-problematic orientation and relatedness to other human beings, not just a presumed mirror facing the light of the mind. It can then be automatically perceived that the goal then is to come to peace with and cease to be in a place of reactivity, fear, conflation, or confusion in relationship with 'the world'. Furthermore, 'the world' normally represents the social framework of other people, and how we orientate and behave toward 'them'.

When I first began to really engage with psychedelic states, there was a deluge of unprocessed, uninvestigated material that came to the surface. Once this material comes up, processing it can seem to be an endless task. Yet, I think that by processing this sort of material, the individual can come to a deeper sense of peace. This is one of the primary values of psychedelics, of being able to consciously go into the intricate, delicate work of self-inquiry and face up to the many aspects of the human self. For many, there is great value in being alone and taking a psychedelic compound as an enema for the mind. It is well reported by people such as Jean Houston in her book, *A Mythic Life,* that the father of gestalt psychotherapy Fritz Perls utilised high doses of LSD in deep and silent self-inquiry to process his own issues and allow himself to flower beyond his own neurosis. He had once told her that his own psycho-therapeutic techniques did not work on himself to that end, and implored her to give him LSD, which she would not do, until he finally took matters into his own hands.

It is also that there are often no set answers or results in the depths of the self, and sometimes the resultant states can be of delusion and confusion, as so much 'stuff' and so many elements can come to the surface to be processed, that it can take days or weeks or even months after ingesting the compound to work through and come to peace with it all. Just by taking psychedelics, not everything that appears to be hindering us is simply given to us on a plate for us to process. I cannot see how there is any necessary progression on any presumed path with these compounds, as what we are dealing with is much less linear and structurally orientated than the linear and goal-orientated human mind. By continuing to seriously take psychedelics, we can be made aware of our own psychosis, which is not always brought out or suddenly catalysed through psychedelics, as it is often a pre-existing condition of repressed notions, subconscious thoughts and the silly washing machine of the monkey mind. The naturally inspired process is then to come to terms with the nature of these thoughts and finally come to peace with them. By deeply accepting, listening, understanding, and integrating the monkey mind we can begin to allow it to quieten, so that it no longer has so much power over us. In so many respects we have to let go and surrender. The apparent problem is if we let go, presumably we are left at the mercy of our own 'irrationalities'. Yet the human mechanism will right itself, align and heal itself, given time and space and conducive conditions. In the modern world, obtaining the necessary time and space to carry out this type of deep inner work is a continuing challenge for many.

The Shadow

The shadow is a Jungian term, said to represent the hidden or unconscious aspects of the self. The shadow is an aspect of unconscious functioning that we are either unaware of or feel unable to change, as it seems like such an inherent part of our makeup. The confrontation with the shadow is the one task we must necessarily fulfil in order to 'individuate', in strictly

Jungian terms. Many people have not even come to terms that they have a shadow at all – often choosing only to project their shadow upon other individuals. We still live in a paradigm where many people fear the Id (Freud's word for the unconscious and instinctual self); they fear the shadow and often unconsciously become a victim to it. Many ways of thinking within Western society strongly propose the line of post-Freudian thinking, which infers that the inner self contains dark and dangerous impulses that must be repressed. Yet, it is not the inner self that contains such impulses. It is the repression and, therefore, distortion of the inner self's expression that has caused a distortion of that force. What scares us most, perhaps, are people who are violent and commit irrational acts without rhyme or reason, and who are often considered to be the very definition of evil. Yet these acts can represent an unconscious catharsis of repressed force, or an errant attempt to somehow heal or process these forces.

Conscious work with the shadow is a most serious work, and I have seen highly aware individuals destroy their lives simply by not being able to own, face up to, and work through their own shadow in maturity, humility, and understanding. At times, I think we must go into the often extreme disorder of internal psychosis in order to purge it from us, but I also think it is important to not let ourselves get carried away in indulgent behaviour that gives credibility to the psychosis, which is what the 'psycho' does. The psycho is only coming to terms with what is occurring for him/her, but does not accept their own issues and only projects, defines, and validates them against the world. The expressions of the inner self can appear like a bull at the gate, kept at bay, yet wanting to come out. Assuming the bull goes through the process of breaking free and kicking off its shackles, after some time it must calm down and will likely just go into the field, eat grass and entertain some cows, which is what it wants. Just so, the inner self wants to come out and play, and the force of its desire to emerge implies acts of great violence or sudden irrationality – yet the true nature of the self is ultimately creative and generative. In order to truly work through internal psychosis, it may at times be necessary to let the apparent bull out of the gate in a way that will not do damage. This requires a conscious intent and an understanding of our own weaknesses, rather than only taking refuge in our strengths. Often this type of act will require a supportive framework of others around us who can at least try to understand our process and be present to us in it.

Conscious catharsis can take many forms. Never underestimate the power of just letting feelings come and expressing them, especially anger, through shouting and screaming (preferably in a place where others cannot hear). I have a friend who screams her head off while driving along the freeway in her car. In bio-energetic therapy, there are certain physical exercises and techniques that are used to allow the person to enact some kind of temper tantrum and realise the cause of their frustrations and repressions, which often are related to deep childhood issues. Crying and laughing are other forms of emotional release and expression which can only be encouraged, but not indulged in. It is wise to be aware of attitudes to such expressions in your local neighbourhood. I once knew a woman who was practising 'dynamic meditation' (a form of meditation developed by the late 20th century Indian philosopher and 'guru' Osho) in her bathtub for a few hours, in which laughing and crying are allowed and encouraged. Her boyfriend called the mental hospital that sent around paramedics who took her to the hospital involuntarily, where she stayed, drugged up, for two weeks.

For the most part, people in Western society do not like to acknowledge any sincere or raw expressions of emotion, as at least on a superficial level; emotions and productivity are seen to be at odds with one another. The Austrian psychiatrist and visionary Wilhelm Reich deemed Western society to be emotionally ill, resulting in what he called 'the emotional plague': the repression of emotions causing various maladjustments, destructiveness, deadening of the life force and various forms of mental illness. The malaise of the West is that individuals are very much co-ordinated with their think-ing processes and are often not at all embedded in their feeling, empathetic, emotional, or aware selves at any other level of being. Western European culture can be seen as quite a 'cold' culture, that is not centred in the emo-tional realm. Therefore, to bring balance to this nature, contact with the warmth of emotions and feelings is necessary. Psychedelics can help people to make contact with their emotions and clarify them, and therefore stim-ulate clear thinking to push through personal issues. Yet, there are many other techniques such as bodywork, breath-work, and psychotherapy that are just as effective for working through such issues.

One way to integrate the feeling and energetic nature with awareness is to lie down or sit up and focus on integrating the feeling nature and bodily awareness. I guess this could be considered a kind of meditation. The purpose of this exercise is just to feel whatever comes up, whether that be pain or shifts in the body, and to simply surrender and 'go with it'. It is just a matter of bringing awareness to whatever blocks are present. This way of focusing attention allows the natural intelligence of the body to heal itself. This simple technique also allows a kind of integration between the feeling, emotional, metaphysical nature and bodily awareness and mind. Of course, for many people, the mind is a machine that never stops, and part of why it doesn't stop is that it doesn't want to give up its influence and power. By coming into contact with our emotional and feeling nature, we can realise more easily that we are not in complete and conscious control of what happens to us, and that much of what happens to us and within us, has its basis in other levels of being, not just the mind.

Western society typically encourages a relative depersonalisation or impersonalisation, as the personal implicitly seems too intricate, involved, and confronting – and does not further the obtainment of a pay cheque or luxury goods. But in the personal, the emotional, the feeling basis of who we are, is the basis of our experience, and the more we tend to our emotional self and express it, the more we can live and experience and make use of our life. Therefore, a path of healing lies in humility and awareness of the collective state of humanity and also the collective issues in different races or cultures. A path of authenticity, humility, and healing has a natural drive, and that is simply to experience less suffering and catalyse more of the good stuff – for all human beings.

Processing and Integrating

'Processing' is a word that can be used to describe processing energies within the bio-energetic field of the body. In the early days of my ingestions of tryptamines, I felt like I was a 'processor' carrying out mathematical computations on behalf of humanity and the planet. At times, there didn't seem to be any personal material being processed at all. A lot of the material being worked through appeared to be of a transpersonal nature in which no personal context was present.

Involuntary physical shaking can represent a profound aspect of processing and letting go. There is a difference between shaking and having a seizure because, very simply, shaking will feel good, while a seizure will feel disturbingly violent. Shaking has often been associated with religious rapture. An obvious reference is the 'Shakers', a Christian puritan religious group, which originally settled in eastern North America. One will also witness total involuntary shaking in faith healer gatherings and in the traditions of the Sangoma healers in South Africa. This shaking represents a form of letting go, in which the bio-electric nature causes the bio-energy to pulse and move through the body, triggering the body to move and spasm, breaking up and releasing holding and tension. This sort of spasming and shaking can occur to many naturally during sexual intercourse and should not be shunned or restricted, as this is how the body and mind are integrating in a form of natural letting go. Indeed, the most essentially powerful nature of orgasm as Reich described it, was one in which two bodies relinquished voluntary movement in order to move as one bodily contraction in a climax of mutual rapture.

It is useful to see that in psychedelic processing all pain is not bad. In many Asian forms of bodywork, for example, the approach is often that of 'no pain, no gain'. It is only by going to the areas of blockage whereby one can release what is inhibiting one's self-expression. In going outside of the known mind, we can often discover pain we did not know we had. This pain indicates dysfunction, yet we can find this pain to be our friend; it has texture and meaning, and it is doing us a favour by communicating to us about our dysfunction. When we feel this pain, we are telling ourselves what we need to do to fulfil our own integrative wholeness, so that we may escape from the deceptions of the propped-up ego and engage into realness and humility. It is normally the case that internal pain needs to be felt in order for us to reap the fruit of pleasure and good feeling.

Of course, pain for its own sake is generally not very useful. This is the kind of ascetic pain that brought penitent medieval Christians to wear hair shirts and whip themselves. The issue here is that this pain does not necessarily transform, and the pain signals themselves only indicate some damage is occurring to the physical body.

Emotional pain in any given process can, of course, be as strong as physical pain, if not stronger. Physical pain can be used to obscure emotional pain, when it is the feeling of emotional pain that can assist in bringing true healing. Those who take razors and cut themselves are often only trying to feel something, even if it is a shallow self-made pain, because they have become numb to their own emotions. That being said, medical science does not typically recognise such emotional pain, as according to medical science the only pain that truly hurts must be physical, and emotional pain is somehow considered to be less real, or perhaps only psychosomatic. Yet for individuals, having loved ones die or going through heartbreak are all kinds of deeper pain that can represent a 'proof' of deeper layers of being than the physical, and this kind of pain can even bring us into profound contact with the soul.

What psychedelics can do is bring to light the dysfunctionality of the Western psyche. Suddenly it is observed that all is perhaps not as it could be. One sees beyond the illusions, the shiny carrots, and the sticks. Most of what ostensibly motivates people can be deemed to be quite facile and ignorant. The narcissism and disconnection of the individual from the truth of their own being and that of others becomes very apparent, and we can then realise the great humour, hypocrisy and heartbreak of our own lives and that of all people living in our world.

The Western culture in particular is not one that encourages 'navel gazing' or self-inquiry. We are implicitly encouraged to base awareness in 'the mind', and to let go of 'the mind' is to enter into or engage with a potentially very messy or confusing realm of thoughts, emotions, and denied feelings – which again is not typically deemed to have value. Taking psychedelics with intent will often move one out of the realm of the mind and into this noisy realm. Many are afraid of drowning in their emotions or in the turbulent tides of collective consciousness.

The problem is that many are not orientated to carrying out such profound inner work, which is the natural result of authentic confrontation with the deep self. I would define a mature intent as one that allows growth, learning, and facilitation through personal obstructions, rather than just seeking immediate fulfilment. An immature intent consists of escape, rather than confrontation and with recreation, rather than inner work. Another form of immaturity that can be commonly observed is where there is predominately a kind of transcendentalism that does not involve or invoke or integrate different levels of the psyche and being (or what is commonly called 'spiritual bypassing').

Low doses of cactus and mushrooms could be used by far more people as psychoactive medicines, whereas low doses of 2C-B or MDMA do not tend to work so well medicinally. However, Albert Hofmann swore by low doses of semi-synthetic LSD at dosages around 25 micrograms. Too often, people are only looking for the mind-manifesting aspects of psychedelics, whereas 'micro dosing', especially with iboga, mushrooms, ayahuasca, cactus, and LSD can affect us in a positive way, beyond our conscious mind, by allowing the psychoactive medicine to carry out healing work upon us while we are still somewhat in our 'normal' state of mind.

Too often people take a dose that is neither high enough nor low enough, but somewhere in between. For LSD to be really interesting, 200 to 500 micrograms is required for most people. For deep work with mushrooms, a good dose is to take 5 to 10 dried grams of mushrooms alone in a dark room. That does not mean that high dosages always need to be taken alone, as the group space can also be useful. Although it sounds very west coast American, I have known people (who were mostly from the west coast in America), who would float each other in a hot tub after having taken a few hundred micrograms of LSD to induce a space of rebirth and the healing that comes from letting go into deep trust with others. Among my friends, it has not been uncommon for us to take cactus together or medium doses of mushrooms. There is an element of revelry in this space, and being together is not entirely humourless or earnest. We have come together and sung, rapped, joked, and enjoyed the opportunity for talk, self-reflection, playing, and being in silence.

So let us not forget the value of pure Dionysianism (Dionysus is a god who represents the enjoyment of revelry, music and inebriation). Much of Western culture is conservative and practically Apollonian (the god Apollo is associated with rationality, order and self-discipline). Diony-sianism has been marginalised and devalued in Western culture as being below Apollonism, so having fun is often not taken very seriously. Parties where people take 'drugs' are often considered to be bad news in North America. North American culture was once so puritan, so Apol-lonian, that it banned alcohol, the drug whereby people loosen up and socialise more easily. Of course, drinking alcohol does not allow you to address why you are so tight or tense, or possibly why you cannot easily communicate and commune with the opposite sex without it!

MDMA is well known as a great tool to improve communication between couples, and for people to communicate more deeply and work through any issues in a relationship. For myself, and others, MDMA has been used to come out of our shell and communicate more openly with people in social situations, and generally get over ourselves and our own issues with so-called 'people'. A lot of this occurred for me at nightclubs or at open-air doof parties where people gather in larger groups. It is not uncommon for people to deliberately take MDMA to work through their own issues, but also people will naturally work through many issues and problems under its influence. For example, as reported in Nicholas Saunders book *E for Ecstasy,* the MDMA boom in late-1980s England effectively ended soccer hooligan-ism. Rather than going out and beating each other up, soccer enthusiasts would take MDMA, and decided that 'loving' each other and enjoying the communal experience of rave parties was better fun than going out into the streets to fight and brawl.

The laughing that people often experience during the psychedelic state is, in itself therapeutic, as laughter is a natural form of catharsis. My recom-mendation is to laugh until there is no more laughing to be had. Nitrous oxide is called 'laughing gas' because it induces certain types of realisation that bring the release and catharsis of laughing. Yet, this laughing is perhaps only a stage that neophytes may go through and not something that experienced psychedelic users will go into regularly. Although, laughter is perhaps one of the most under-rated cathartic processes, and sometimes it can be hard to know exactly what you are laughing about, only that deep realisations and releases are occurring.

My experience with nitrous-oxide (laughing gas) is that it increases a circulation of sorts. There are then certain types of communication and sub-communications that occur within consciousness when there is too much circulation and stress within the body. When this circulation is increased to a certain point, the body's response seems to be to create a mystical experience as a type of reward. However, I find there is a limit to how far I can get tricked. My body just tells me there is too much circulation here and it is stressing and possibly damaging the body. There are certain signals and patterns and cues pertaining to my body's own sophisticated channels of communication with itself that I then begin to witness, and the realisation of the sophistication of this internal system of communication brings laughter.

The ingestion of psychedelic compounds can only potentially facilitate a mystical experience, but not guarantee it. There are so many possibilities for profound realisation and transformation within the dreaming state, but every dream you have is not always going to be profound and life-changing. My understanding is that dreams represent a way in which we can receive communications from a deeper place of intelligence than our conscious mind, but these communications do not need to occur every night. Just because you have taken a psychedelic compound does not guarantee anything will happen. At times, especially with the synthetic chemicals, what will be experienced is just a whole lot of noise. It also becomes clear that awareness exists within certain boundaries; especially when 'coming back' from certain states, it becomes obvious that some information is not going to be retained in the waking state. This cannot be emphasised enough. The human state is more or less one of limitation and, in a sense, that is its value. It is useful to realise that this limitation can encourage us to focus in certain ways that are beneficial to what we are.

Feeching, Sound Navigation and Telepathy

What I call 'feeching' is a process of attempting to let go of the jaw, allowing the jaw to vibrate of its own accord. This involuntary vibratory movement of the jaw first became apparent to me when I began taking MDMA. I also noticed when I practised high frequency singing, that by letting go of the jaw, I could make a whole range of shifting frequencies that could not be made voluntarily. This letting go of the jaw is involuntary and very similar to the letting go in the hips and pelvis that Wilhelm Reich communicates of, in which there is an involuntary contraction and movement of the pelvis during the contractions of orgasm. It is via this type of letting go, that we can release the mind and get back into an integrated awareness of the body.

Through feeching, I found I was able to release fear from deep within my bio-energetic system. At times, I can literally feel a release in specific parts of the body whether that be in the throat, the stomach, the shoulders, or in other parts of the body. What is normally being released can feel like a kind of fear or contraction, cold or stagnant energy.

This is a short video I made which demonstrates feeching:

https://www.youtube.com/watch?v=pwvAOneTLGM

When I first began taking synthetic phenethylamines, I noticed they allowed me to go into feeching for hours at a time when normally half an hour was an exceptional length of time to be doing this. In my regular state, there was a limit to the amount of time I could feech, and then there was no more to process. Much of my early enthusiasm regarding synthetic phenethylamines was perhaps simply their ability to allow this feeching and the resulting states of well-being and good feeling. Feeching then also occurred for me in heightened states such as during sexual intercourse or under a waterfall absorbing negative ions or swimming in the surf.

Sound is one of the primary ways to guide the psychedelic experience, so being able to make sound and tone is a useful skill to know. Whether that sound is toning, or grunting, or moaning, or making 'oohh' or 'aahh' sounds, it is just letting oneself 'play' and just making the sounds that is perhaps the most important thing. High-pitched sounds can be made and different pitches of sound can be produced at the same time, similar to Tuvan throat singing. It is really quite bizarre what sounds are expressed when you just let yourself go into it. The effects that higher frequency sounds can have are quite profound, and I often feel a vibratory shuddering in my brain after singing. Some people, including myself, can often sing delightful songs off the top of their head after taking mushrooms or ayahuasca.

Sounding or toning is a good way to access emotion, to communicate and express and process internal realities. Yet, it is not by singing known songs necessarily that we can do this. It is quite common for people to channel songs that are sung in an unknown or even alien language. Once after taking a few dried grams of mushrooms, I was met by an inter-dimensional being that took over my vocal chords and proceeded to have a kind of intercourse with me, with the singing being a carrier medium for this connection. This being was docking into me quite intricately, with quite startling visuals of shape-shifting cords and tentacles. The feeling and experience was rich and good, but not particularly organic or 'sexual'. It was a form of communion not related to the genitals or even any aspect of my bio-energetic anatomy I was aware of.

Channelling other beings does and can happen in the psychedelic state, and they do sometimes take over your vocal chords and begin speaking. I would say it is nothing to be afraid of, but nothing to take too seriously. Among psychics, 'trance channelling', where the person is giving their body over to another entity to speak through them, is often heavily discouraged. There are many books in the marketplace written by entities that speak through the body of a human being to share words of wisdom. The Seth books channeled by Jane Roberts are perhaps the most expansive and mind opening of all these works. I would say, however, it seems to be more vital to find one's own voice, even one's own songs, which will tend to come through of their own accord through letting go.

I know a woman who spoke fluent Portuguese during an ayahuasca group, even though she had never spoken Portuguese before in her life. The session was facilitated by a Brazilian woman who, of course, understood what she was saying. It is also not uncommon for people to speak or sing in a new language after taking tryptamines like psilocybin mushrooms or ayahuasca. Sometimes these apparently new languages are not dissimilar to glossolalia; sometimes they can appear as an alien language or just some kind of mindless blather. Sometimes English words are transformed to apparently have two, three, four, or even more meanings and thus resemble complicated 'puns'. The point is that meaning is communicated via words, but the structure of language can be stretched in order to accommodate a vaster range of possible meanings.

When there is openness and meaning present, direct telepathy is possible, in and out of psychedelic states. It is simply a matter of being open to others reading your mind, and reading the minds of others. Telepathy is not a sign of schizophrenia, rather, it is a sign of a more developed framework of beingness than the Western status quo. Australian Aboriginal people are quite well known to practice telepathy, even when they are far apart from each other. Indeed, it is possible to be telepathic with another person when the physical body of that person is not present. What you are communicating with could be understood as their over-self, their unconscious, or their higher self. For all extents and purposes, the person looks the same and sounds the same as the person you know. The communications you can have in this state can really get to the essence of a matter or business you may have with them, and may point out transpersonal issues or understandings that can allow many core elements to be worked through in a dynamic. I once even ended up doing marriage counselling for a couple one day when I was walking along the beach alone. A middle-aged Aboriginal lady saw me, stopped dead in her tracks, mouth open, then smiled and said, "Good onya fella!"

During my work with ayahuasca, I was often in dialogue with specific beings or specific people, and a story unfolded. Then I would go with the story, as a metaphor if you like. Sometimes this story can appear to be imaginal, in that the imagination appears to be creating a story. Yet, the data is the data. You engage with it and in letting go, in suspending disbelief and belief; you take the ride of the experience. In operating this way you often feel that you are changing and transforming levels of reality at an archetypal level. At the same time, you can become aware of deeper levels of reality and engage in dialogue with the underlying elements within that reality. At times, it can become confusing as to what is actually the case. To start talking about these levels of reality 'as' reality is likely going to confuse a lot of people and yourself. Sometimes it takes a lot of reflection to understand what is truly the case. What may often be experienced is of a different dimensionality and can appear quite wild. Many of these states can become a kind of work, as sometimes it seems that certain data needs to be crunched and processed. Oftentimes this data can appear as raw code. Or it can appear as teams of rabid men and women dressed in garish swimming costumes that you are trying to convince not to vomit on one another! It is often that random.

When working with this sort of material, it is vital to allow oneself to go into what wants to happen, letting go of control of the normal and usual neuro-linguistic pathways. This often requires a letting go of one's identity, which typically tends to be inhibitive and somewhat self-important. This is not always an easy thing to do, but necessary if we are to be actively free of our own tendencies to imprison ourselves and inhibit the range of expression of our own essential nature.

The Guide

For many people in the 1960s, the LSD state was a new territory, and many chose to experience that state with the help of a guide. But is the psychedelic guide really necessary or helpful? My view is that if people feel activated in this capacity, then it can be useful to have them present in that capacity. I once took a friend around the small tourist town of Byron Bay after he had taken LSD. It was clear he did not want to see what I wanted to show him. I had often taken psychedelics in this seaside town, and I wanted him to see the kind of material he would see, because I had seen it. He later said what he saw was the raw reality of people, without mental contextualisations, illusions, and excessive mentation. In this raw perception, he was able to see their suffering, their emotions, their masks, their hopes, their joy – as if it was seen for the first time, so much so that it appeared to be a entirely different perspective of reality, but it was only an acute perspective of present reality, outside of the buffers of the mind and cultural programming. I literally had to hold my friend's hand and shepherd him into facing the people and stop him from walking away. Sometimes I would speak in a poetic way, confirming what I knew he was seeing and putting it into context, helping him on his journey through this raw human reality with open eyes. I have also met a man who works with psychoactive plants, who sometimes gives his 'clients' a decent amount of cactus juice and takes them walking in the mall.

From *The Psychedelic Experience* by Timothy Leary, Ralph Metzner and Richard Alpert, it is written about the guide:

> "The key issue here is the guide's ability to turn off his own ego and social games – in particular, to muffle his own power needs and his fears. To be there relaxed, solid, accepting, secure. The Tao wisdom of creative quietism. To sense all and do nothing except to let the subject know your wise presence."

There is a small and underground movement, largely in North America and Europe, of people who use psychedelics within the context of guided psychotherapy sessions, often within a group context. Besides this, psychedelic guides are not quite as prevalent as they once were in the 1960s and 70s. I do not think we should necessarily consider the guide to be superior to shared experience and exploration, but when people are just starting out, having a good guide can be very useful in order to begin to make friends with these states.

Much can also be said for experiencing the psychedelic world by yourself. Even a substance like 2C-B or Foxy (5-MeO-DiPT), which many people utilise to enhance lovemaking, can be beneficial to take alone. But it must be said that so much fruit can be borne in relating in the psychedelic state – and it is not just in sexual intercourse, although there is that. Men, for example, can find sexual potentials they did not know they had, like the ability to have multiple orgasm without ejaculating. And once that experience is reached, there a true reference point for it to occur again.

Mebbing and Sex

When I first began to take psychedelics, I realised that the metaphysical dynamic and potential alchemy between the masculine and the feminine was fundamental and seemingly overlooked by so many. It appeared to me that people weren't truly respecting or bringing forth any fruit from this metaphysical dynamic. I knew that there could often be powerful energies in sex, but that was not what I was looking for. I knew my answer was not 'love' – either 'falling in love' or this concept bandied around me so commonly, but with more talk than walk, it seemed to me. I was looking for something else. What I was seeking was a depth, a communion I felt was never really offered to me in my culture. Yet, I did begin to find it, and then realised the energetic dimensions of relationships that can become apparent. I had tastes of this energetic communion mostly in embraces with women, in a hug, which often became something like a mystical experience. This was however quite rare, although other people have told me they had the same experience, where an apparently casual hug became something much, much larger than that.

I began to experience what I was seeking, and it was a state that could just happen with little physical proximity at all. It was a kind of overwhelming intimacy itself; however anytime I touched it, it seemed like it was too much to handle. Then I met an extraordinary woman, just as experienced with powerful psychedelics as myself, who was versed in telepathy. Being with her was far beyond psychedelics, and we never had sex. The few concentrated days during which we shared timelessness were a true validation. It was then a year before I found a girl who was truthful, honest and open on that level, and I felt such love for her. We took acid and MDMA on the beach and jumped up and down in excitement about coming together.

Then, I had another girlfriend for five years, who was actually very blocked to intimacy. Being with her was a struggle, a challenge to actually get through to her, but I tuned my radio, my frequency, to her frequency. I spent many hundreds of hours just holding her (I don't like to use the word 'cuddling', as it sounds so soft and ineffectual). After we parted, I had experiences with other women that solidified this understanding and practice.

Often this involved being in a psychedelic state and just holding a woman, front to front. This would enable energetic and psychic transmission that could become very strong. I understood how females were very different, that their energy and level of openness was different as well as the way they related through energy, so the consequent communion and its nature was also very different.

I had experiences of orgasm and deep pleasure that went far beyond the feeling of some semen squirting out of the end of my penis. I had experiences of magical connection that exceeded most of my psychedelic experiences. I had profound understandings of what the female orgasm is and how to bring it about, and most importantly, what it meant. After I broke up with my girlfriend, I used to hold her, and we would go deeper than we ever did in five years of lovemaking. I had realised a way of mystical connection and healing, which I did not see any obvious reference to in Western Tantra or in any Eastern tradition. Suddenly, this had become a kind of ritual of its own kind – the key to unlocking the nature and meaning of human sexuality was to simply relate, not through the sexual circuitry, but via simple intentionality. Relating seriously in this way was like meditation on steroids, but, instead of one person sitting on top of the mountain alone, there were two people facing each other to realise unity. I thought of a word, 'mebbing', wrote a 4,000-word essay, and created a web site:

http://www.mebbing.org

These days I find mebbing puts me in a visionary psychedelic state which is as potent as taking a decent dose of mushrooms. I believe mebbing to be a very useful experience and a healthy response to the lack of intimacy in Western society and most modern day approaches to sexuality. Through mebbing, I think people can realise that the primary meat and meaning of relationship is an energetic dynamic, which can be practised and in which there is much possible fruit.

In terms of sex and psychedelics, I personally feel that sex is deep enough and powerful enough on its own and, in fact, I always found psychedelics and sex to be too powerful to deal with. But in this heightened state, many people can awaken an understanding of the deeper energies and possibilities of intimacy involved in sex and relating.

However, many men only experience the primary value of sexuality in terms of the pleasure that occurs in ejaculation. The basis of modern day 'Tantric' sexual practices can be summed up by saying it involves the man contracting his PC muscle so as to delay his squirting orgasm in order to experience deeper pleasure in connection and hopefully, to deliver the female orgasm, as well as a deeper and more energising orgasm for himself. Yet, the female orgasm is not just for herself – the man should experience pleasure from it as well. In fact, he is energetically empowered by her orgasm, when he is present enough that she feels she can connect with him. The most essential nature of the female orgasm is when she energetically connects to him. In a sense, her orgasm is emotional, but it is also energetic, and can occur with total strangers if there is a natural resonance between them.

Doris Lessing from *The Golden Notebook* writes:

> "A vaginal orgasm is emotion and nothing else, felt as emotion and expressed in sensations that are indistinguishable from emotion. The vaginal orgasm is a dissolving in a vague, dark generalised sensation like being swirled in a warm whirlpool. There are several different sorts of clitoral orgasms, and they are more powerful (that is a male word) than the vaginal orgasm. There can be a thousand thrills, sensations, etc. but there is only one real female orgasm and that is when a man, from the whole of his need and desire takes a woman and wants all her response. Everything else is a substitute and a fake and even the most inexperienced woman feels this instinctively."

So the female orgasm is very important. In fact, female sexuality is vitally important, because men can become men through it, as the female innately defines man through this act. It is not necessarily that when she is having an orgasm, he is stealing her energy (as the olden day Chinese Taoists thought), or that she is giving him energy. It is that she is awakening his energy system; she is defining it, just as he is awakening her as a woman. For her sexual interactions to be truly meaningful, there may be primary issues that the woman needs to work through. She may have been sexually abused in her past. She may have had inattentive or selfish lovers who could not satisfy her. She may just be numb or not had an orgasm through penetration, or very simply, she may just not understand that sex can be much more than mutual masturbation, but can be an act of relationship, connection, love, and celebration.

There are practices such as the 'G spot massage' and the 'Tantric massage' that aim to allow the woman to work through her sexual issues and become sexually activated. When she is sexually activated, he is sexually activated, and he is sexually activated only if that is his intention. Or he may want to continue, to 'piss in women', as Wilhelm Reich said, as if that was 'macho'. There is also a practice called Tantric massage for men, which can allows men to understand how to delay ejaculation via a woman helping them to delay ejaculation with her hands.

Mushrooms are probably the most effective psychedelic agent for engaging in sex. Sex on ayahuasca has been described as simply the realisation that two bodies moving are actually one body. I have heard of entire communities of people that exist on the premise of having sex on psychedelics, so this is of course, a compelling area for many.

Chapter Nine

This Time and These Experiences

Exploring New Age Transpersonalism

Much of the psychedelic ethos that predominates in the West tends to perpetuate what transpersonal theorist Gregg Lahood calls *New Age Transpersonalism*, a phenomenon he describes as having its roots in late 1960s North America.

> "A complex spiritual revolution took place in America in which 'transcendence' became a central orientation. This revolution, while successful in stopping the war, sets the scene for the emergence of non-relational transpersonal psychology (centred in the cosmos beyond human needs a la Maslow) in which Americanised non-dualism gains ascendency. Recent critiques have suggested that popular transpersonalism traps the spirit in a subtle Cartesian prison, a structure that can breed a self-serving, 'self-as-everything' form of spiritual narcissism.

> But just what beliefs do have currency in New Age Transpersonalism? This is a very difficult question to answer but very briefly, two anthropologists David Young and Jean-Guy Goulet suggest that the New Age is a religion and it tends to view reality in terms of different dimensions, and enlightenment

as a movement to ever higher dimensions [of consciousness], either in this life or in lives to come. (Young & Goulet 1994) Reality, according to the perennial philosophy, writes Ken Wilber, is composed of several different but continuous dimensions.

New Age religion joins psychology and religion with a millenarian impulse (the coming of: a New Age of Aquarius, Total Bliss, the coming of the Cosmic Christ, 2012 etc) and an evolutionary design, the result is a self-oriented spirituality in which the transformation of, or the attainment of, a higher inner self is of paramount importance. Furthermore, for many, the action of expanding one's consciousness is deemed an activity that can 'save the planet' (this means, of course, that everyone on the planet must participate in the consciousness raising). New Age religion advocates a perennial philosophy stressing the transcendent unity of all religions although it expresses a religious metaphysic that reflects a Hindu/Gnostic, impersonal, non-dual, transcendentalism."

Personally, I am not into New Age bashing because any technique, any philosophy, any metaphysically orientated practice that is not obviously religious, can be thrown into this very large basket. It is also that New Agers are hard to come by, as pretty much nobody confesses to being a New Ager.

As Gregg Lahood stated in a personal communication in early January 2014:

"I wrote the paper as an aetiology of a psychocultural malady, a kind of liberation for myself and hopefully others. As a New Ager I would be bashing myself. The thing about New Agers in my opinion is that it's very hard to find one, unlike McKenna's (a rabid New Ager) butterflies they are about as hard to pin down as an angel. So I hereby confess to be such a one, albeit a recovering New Ager."

In the West, since the late 1960s, some potentially very valuable techniques and practices for health, healing, and well-being have been developed. For many, acupuncture is 'new age', yet in many parts of Asia, acupuncture is simply a treatment utilised for thousands of years to heal the body and alleviate suffering in hundreds of millions of people. In the West, many would like to rein in acupuncture via a kind of cultural imperialism, whereby anything that doesn't accord with Western scientific materialistic perspectives must be judged on those terms, rather than even slightly engaged with on its own terms. Rather than accepting that Easterners are not deluding themselves as to the existence of meridians that influence 'chi' via needles, Western skeptics would prefer to claim the impossibility of these observations and oppose any system of understanding that does not conform to their purely physical-materialist worldview.

I think it is quite evident that many so-called skeptics are loath to embrace techniques designed to get the Western mind out of the head and into the body. The simple truth is that the skeptics are often those who have most investment in the traditional structures of the exclusively intellectual mind. Therefore, these folks commonly take a lot of pride in their practice of rationality or logic, and obviously feel a need to deride anything that appears to threaten the hegemony of their investment in these intellectual paradigms. At the root of this protestation, is the essentially Western predilection to resist feeling, to resist the internal metaphysical dimensions of life and maintain the life of 'the mind' as the only life. Yet it is only through feeling that the soul is known. Prideful, excessively left brained skeptics are very often averse to acknowledging they are handicapped when it comes to appropriating the internal and feeling dimensions. Because in my perception, such people tend to not often focus, deal with or integrate the right brained aspects of their psyche. This aspect of their being is often not well developed, meaning they can be highly irrational people, and are often very fearful of truly facing their own crazy emotional immaturity. This entire idealogical enterprise of so-called skepticism seems to me to be a defensive procedure of denial, born out of profound insecurity, designed to maintain the locus of the mind and deny feeling levels of reality and therefore, anything metaphysical that may imply the existence of the soul.

Perhaps this tendency to bring awareness back to the mind at all times emerges because of the potential challenges that occur when awareness moves out of the presently known intellectual maps. What many people are essentially afraid of is facing themselves in their own field of essential truth, in their own being. Western intellectual thought can often encourage a kind of mental masturbation – namely the recirculation of the same thoughts rehashed and disconnected from any kind of actual internal and human basis, and this is the common enough dissociation of intellectual academic thought.

I have participated in group breathwork sessions with the esteemed Dr. Lahood and I believe that breathwork is one of the most effective ways I have witnessed for people to make deep contact with their somatic body beyond their mind. Breathwork is also an effective way to bear witness to your own pain and therefore your own bliss. Yet, no such ecstasies are typically allowed for the self-appointed automatons of consumerism, and many consumers would perhaps consider breathwork 'New Age'. Some people consider any perspective that admits any kind of inner self, apart from the stripped back body and mind, to be 'New Age', which is considered to be akin to witchcraft, practiced by the foolish and deluded. Perhaps part of this is that New Agers admit an internal reality which many would like to consider to be unreal, so 'they' can often be cynically considered to be kooks, crackpots, cranks, and charlatans only out for the quick buck.

What I do perceive in the West, is simply the denial of realities other than those that we have apparent control of. In response to so-called 'fluffy' and 'soft' New Agers, we get hardened intellectual rigorousness, as if that is a panacea. At the end of the day, I do think that the term 'New Age' is really quite silly and redundant, creating more of a rigid sense of 'us' and 'them' than is really necessary. In an ailing cultural ethos, my perception is that there are people who have a natural ability to access to non-physical realities, and those who do not. Those who do authentically have that access are often not likely to be involved in the New Age, but are more likely to be in mental hospitals or having trouble being sensitive and aware in a desensitised and brazen culture, perhaps finding solace in drugs like alcohol or heroin. People I know who have had or do have any kind of natural and direct access to other realities, beings, or just a profound contact with their own soul awareness and that of others, normally have quite a lot of difficulty with it. I have often found psychics to be quite troubled people, continually trying to cope with an awareness of the glaring fractures they perceive in the lives of themselves and others.

The New Age market in the West is typically considered by marketers to be dominated by married woman in their 40s and 50s who, having raised children, are seeking greater meaning in their lives. Many people who could be considered to be New Agers are retired people who are seeking a way to access spirituality and meaning in their lives. I think it is quite clear to see, that many Western cultural archetypal identities are quite shallow and superficial. An individual in Western culture is at times called on to identify with a cultural archetype, so that we are able to identify each other and our apparent cultural role from 100 yards away.

I have observed that most so-called New Agers do not easily admit an ailing cultural ethos, but perpetuate the dominant cultural ethos as that of the norm. For example, in the world of Western Tantra, the work of Wilhelm Reich is largely unknown or seemingly only superficially under- stood. Reich's understanding of the true and essential nature of orgasm basically negates much of Western Tantra, because Reich stated that the fundamental principle of orgasm was a complete vibratory communion in which the two bodies engage into involuntary convulsions and become one. The sexualised version of popular Western Tantra is, for the most part, glorified or 'sacred' fucking, stressing the narcissism of orgasm and 'pleasure', often without the kind of surrender into organic connection and union that Reich stated as being fundamental. Indeed, Western Tantra is often inclined to focus on techniques that at times often serve to fascinate the mind, titillate the body, and glorify the ego.

Similarily, in the psychedelic movement, there can be quite a juvenile el- ement, which prioritises the 'mind candy' in psychedelic experiences. In traditional eastern religions, the initiate is typically told to go beyond all phenomena. As a religion, Christianity seems to give more value to human relationships: the summation of the teachings of St. John on his deathbed at an ancient age was only to 'love one another'. Most religions stress the relationship between the individual and the numinous, whether that be god or the clear light. In that sense, perhaps all religions represent a kind of 'New Age Transpersonalism', stressing vertical rather than horizontal transcendence. This tendency perhaps only reflects the syncretic 'metaphysique' of the new age which draws inspiration from all religions, eastern and western.

As Gregg Lahood states:

> "Furthermore the New Age has been described as spiritual consumerism (Arweck 2002) in a pick n' mix, spiritual marketplace (Roof 1996). Once counter-cultural, the New Age sanctifies capitalism (Mikaelsson 2003) and promulgates a search (journey) for prosperity and a means to wealth (Morris 2006). Spirituality has in a sense become a 'commodity'; a fetish linked to purchasing power and economically based self-esteem. Lavish spending on spiritual commodities (eg. expensive New Age group events, spiritual tourism or showy donations to gurus buy power and participation mystique (without the transmutative suffering required to reduce narcissistic alienation). This kind of conspicuous consumption may also be intended to create envy in others – (there is perhaps nothing of more value to the spiritual egoist than the envy of others)."

The relative popularity of ayahuasca in the West, with its marketing of illusions and high price tags, perhaps typifies the kind of consumerism Lahood writes of. However, even though there are elements of narcissism in Western spiritual seeking, it is clear that many are simply attempting to discover the sacred in themselves – a sense of soul or even the soul itself. But what Lahood talks of here as a remedy ('transmutative suffering') is really about feeling and then understanding the dysfunction that prevents contact with the soul, or true self. Suffering is often transmutative, as suffering is the messaging mechanism that something is wrong, and these sensations of suffering can allow the body to realise what actually needs to be fixed.

I have observed that the English speaking cultures promote two primary taboos in their operating systems – that of functioning in an apparently foolish manner, and secondly, personally operating and being directed from an internal basis or authority rather than by the obvious terms of the cultural operating system. Yet, foolishness is only the resulting state that arises from exploring the new. Doing something for the first time is quite often frowned upon in traditional conservative frameworks, because you are not likely to get it right and this could severely affect your bank balance. In the higher echelons of any field, 'not getting it right' is frowned upon severely. The surest way to do something wrong is to try and carry out something new, to explore and experiment. Nonetheless, entrepreneurs, inventors, and the like, are the individuals who are most likely to put themselves out on a limb to do a new thing, and this ability to overcome such challenges is often what will make them money. It is in exploring and experimenting where innovations and fresh insights happen, but also in this newness is where you are commonly going to make the most mistakes, be the most challenged, but also learn the most.

The English language itself does not allow for too much internal investigation. We are typically only allowed demure naval-gazing, and 'finding oneself' is commonly ridiculed by British comics. There is very little internal reality the English allow for each other, apart from the known mental realm of domination and control. That there are other innate facilities of awareness apart from the mind, can often seem absurd to those strongly embedded within the modus operandi of English/Anglo culture. Psychedelics can take one both into the internal world and into many possible realms of foolishness. When properly transported, one must look at the world afresh and at everything in fresh and new terms. Any resulting foolish outburst is paradoxically necessary and yet socially forbidden, as nobody appears to want to deal with fresh data that is often the present moment truth. It is apparently much easier to crunch the old data and play by the well-known rules, and in that case, one can possibly 'win' the game, or survive it unscathed. To suggest new data is to break the rules. In the West (and indeed in most cultures), we normally don't like people who suggest new data or that a world view might require changing. Of course, very rarely, has any innovation in world-view not been extremely threatening to the status quo.

Emotion itself is often also considered foolish for the English, so it is then considered best to stay buttoned down and keep that upper lip very stiff, and the cold fish under your collar unflappable. Yet, there is so much richness in the reality of the inner world that does not conform to the understandings or limitations of reductionism or scientific materialistic paradigms – which are only certain convenient descriptions of reality that men have very recently developed. Many forget this because they do not typically choose to observe the realm of man from outside of the realm of man – such is our collective egocentric narcissism.

The term 'New Age' is often used as a standard throwaway euphemism for 'foolishness', which is not quite correct. 'New Age' thought is often as arrogant, reductionistically symbolic, systemised, and exclusively 'mental' as any other style of western thought. There is normally little 'foolishness' in it, little space for the new, challenging, contrary, or authentically artistic. And it is not that New Age people are some coherent tribe, all of whom have surrendered their minds to the truthful inner reality of their thoughts and emotions, or have become emotionally un-armoured in a Reichian sense. Nor are 'they' a group of people fearlessly exploring the new – quite the contrary, in fact. Our fundamental way of operating in the West is typically through an exclusively mental domination of reality. If we want to find truly heart-centred or 'foolish' people, we must go east or south of Western Europe. Many heart-centred or foolish people in Western culture tend to be homeless, as we apparently have no place for people who are not entirely mentally distracted, or do not agree to abide by often quite petty rules and precepts.

Having lived in something of a New Age mecca Byron Bay, Australia, for 11 years, I felt there were very few individuals at peace or happy embedded in such cultures. Fundamental to this discontent I think is the tendency to see thought itself, or thinking, as the most fundamental means to perceive and understand reality. I believe this tendency is the primary error of the Western mindset, of which the New Age is just another subset. The so-called New Age religion can simply present more mental traps in exactly the same manner that religions do. These religious forms are, at the end of the day, not foolishly explorative or particularly accurate regarding the expanse of other realities – and that is why the psychedelic world and the New Age one are not particularly close cousins. There is just as much reductionism in New Age thought as in other forms of Western thought, and there is the same power attributed to symbolic forms or technology of thought. There is the same arrogance of undue understanding, with all the merkabas, flowers of life, OM's, higher selves, "ascended masters" – and the lingo and cosmology is complete. New Agers very often dislike being challenged by a vacuum, or that they may not know exactly how reality is, just as much as scientific materialists often hate the same kind of uncertainty. We can observe the same obsession with self-congratulatory mental forms that distract us from feeling, being present, intuitive, empathic and authentic in moment-to-moment, relevant reality. The New Age flake is the kissing cousin of the absent-minded scientist.

The Follies and Pitfalls of Shamanism

So if we do not wear the feather from the bird of the indigenous tribe, and we do not sing their songs in the style they sing, wear their clothes and smoke their herbs through their pipes, then what do we do? I would say we are then in a place of zero point, in a place where we do not have to conform to the strict unfolding of a story or mythology, and are free to create how we want all this to go. Rather than looking backwards to the past and retelling the stories that have been told before, we can look toward the future, explore new territory, and make new pathways into primordial artistry. That does not mean we must forsake the past, but always referring to the past is not to be true to what could be deemed the essential nature of reality either. This is the reality often spoken of by indigenous people, in which past, future, and present are perceived to be one.

Typically, what you will hear in the West is that you need a 'shaman' if you want to ingest psychoactive plants. This is perhaps an over-conservative perspective, as you do not necessarily need a shaman. However, taking these plants can take you through some tricky territory, and it is not entirely riskless. Many potential pitfalls present themselves when you open up to the spirit world. But just as rock climbing can be extremely dangerous, this does not mean that people should be prevented from rock climbing if that is their desire. When a rock climber accidentally dies, all the other rock climbers do not stop rock climbing, and laws are not introduced to ban rock climbing. So it is that these psychoactive plants can catalyse us into very tricky territory, but also a challenging territory, that can make us all the better for taking the journey, for taking the risks implicit in that journey.

I have always liked to journey alone, outside in nature, so I can make as much sound as I like and not disturb anyone. But in my first forays with many compounds, I always had a sitter who was there for me and that is, I think, a very simple and necessary measure for people who are just start-ing out. Some people will say that you need a shaman present who will protect you from the dark spirits. In the first instance, many shamans are not as adept in the spirit realm as Westerners would like to think, and are often quite hands-off when it comes to 'dark spirits' and the various types of extreme craziness gringos can often bring to the fore. I have heard that a well-regarded shaman in Peru, when several people during his session became overcome by what he said were their own demons, simply hogtied them and put bandanas over their mouths, so they could not disturb the other people present. Also, dark sorcery is so prevalent in the Amazon among curanderos that it may well be the malevolent machinations of the shaman that becomes the primary problem for many people.

But let us also not forget that possession could be perceived to be just as common by those who do not take any psychedelic plants. There is actually a shortage of trained exorcists in the world at this time. That being said, I have not heard of a confirmed permanent possession occurring through the use of psychedelic plants, but that does not mean it has not happened or cannot happen. Almost everyone knows of someone who has burnt out or who 'never came back', or at least, people who changed in many ways, putting them out balance; yet, this usually happens with LSD or research chemicals. This issue is also not so cut and dry. There are many forces and realities in the human world and they actually always influence us. So when it comes to malevolent spirits, they can be overstated, or become an irrational and fear-based obsession. They can be influential and many will say, well, they don't exist at all. I would say that most cultures recognise the existence of spirits and the spirit world and it is largely only modern day Western culture that does not recognise spirits.

As well as good spirits whose effects are felt to be good, there are bad spirits whose effects are felt to be bad. Some will say, well, children experience monsters under the bed, but that doesn't make them real. And I would say, well, the children are scared of the monsters – but no child has ever died of a monster attacking them from under the bed. In my experience, it is often that the worst dark spirits can do is distract you or influence you in ways that could be to your detriment. But I also think individuals must ask themselves what they are doing to deal with these potential influences – and understand they can be dealt with. Also, we must remember, when under the influence, that we can become much more influenced than when in a sober state. This has the potential to have very dangerous consequences even for those who like to think of themselves as strong minded. This is why a sitter is especially imperative for those first starting out ingesting psychedelic plants or compounds. And even for very experienced people, it is not to say that journeying alone is as dangerous as rock climbing alone, but it has its perils. Many beginners vastly understate the power of these materials. We are often dealing with extremely serious states, that our cultural upbringing has simply not prepared us to deal with. We can often expect unexamined, toxic, neurotic, and inexplicable mental, psychic and emotional states to come to the surface, that can be overwhelming for many people and cause them to completely spin out. This is especially the case with synthetic compounds and also with LSD. It is not that LSD or these compounds are inherently dangerous, but that if you are going to take these compounds, especially for the first time, it is absolutely necessary to have someone present as a sitter, to keep you out of potential trouble. This is not a hard thing to arrange, to simply be present as an anchor to another person, and then that person can do the same for you at another time.

There are a few stories on the internet of people beginning to journey alone and then ending up calling the paramedics. I have had to convince a housemate not to call the paramedics after he took a decent amount of mushrooms alone in his room for self-inquiry without telling me. I ended up sitting for him, but a few hours later when I thought he had stabilised, he proceeded to throw a cat on my knee from across the room and then pour water over my head as I comforted the cat!

This is the fear of many people, that they will 'lose it' and become out of control. A key point here is not that people commonly go into a psychotic or schizophrenic states, although that can happen. More likely what is happening is that underlying psychotic or repressed thoughts come to the fore of one's psyche. Therefore, it is most vital to apprehend and understand the potential value of working through one's underlying insanity. I have been through purgative processes that looked psychotic to others around me. What seems most apparent to me is that psychosis and neurosis is commonly repressed in Western people. Also, I can say at this point that I feel incredibly sane. I do not have any fear of losing control or going out of my mind because there is no mind to go out of. I understand it is very possible to realise a more essential rudder or foundation for being, than the mind or the ego, which by nature are incredibly insecure in any of their fragile positionalities.

In the West, of course, we are still a nascent culture when it comes to psychedelics. Collectively, we have not come to terms with how to deal with the immensity of the spirit world. I am not claiming there is a final answer present here. I know of no magic remedy for dealing with malevolent spirits, just as I know of no magic remedy for dealing with difficult or troubling people in day-to-day life. Just as troubling or difficult people can be grist for the mill, so can dark spirits. They can often define one's journey, just as difficult or troublesome people, or your apparent enemies can define your resourcefulness and abilities. It could also be said that shamanism would not exist without dark spirits. If there were only good spirits, for what purpose would the traditional shaman ever be needed?

However, I have found that malevolent spirits can normally be defeated through sound. I find very loud, short, and sharp sounds work very well and can even destroy them. Just through singing for ten to fifteen minutes, each of us will find that with intention and letting go, we will have the sounds that will neutralise pretty much any negative forces. I know other people who say that commanding malevolent spirits to leave in a very firm voice three times works well for them, and many people invoke higher powers such as archangels or helper beings in order to dispel such entities. The spaces we can go into here with these plants are not kidding around, to say the least. It is vital to be very serious and clear in your focus, and ask for guidance and assistance from benevolent spirits when necessary.

So I think each individual has to find their own way here, and I do not recommend that individuals completely buy into the 'protection racket' that is often modern day shamanism. True empowerment and learning is more useful for those inclined to true independence. This attitude involves having a mature and responsible approach that lies in taking responsibility for what becomes apparent. I believe that a more 'psychiatric' rather than 'shamanistic' approach, in seeing the psychological causation of whatever phenomenon is present, is more useful than always dealing with the phenomena on its own terms, without looking into their primary psychological cause. I find that keeping my nose clean, as it were, is the best way to keep ahead of the 'competition' and not be subject to lower level forces – and that is true just as much in my daily life as it is when drinking ayahuasca. In a lot of journeys, it is likely you will never encounter any malevolent beings, and many people with extensive experience with psychedelics have never encountered them. I think its important that each of us take responsibility for any energies or spirits we are attracting to ourselves, and these entities can, at the end of the day, be perceived as part of the play of duality.

It is often that the ayahuascaro is seen as a miracle worker. Yet, when it comes to ayahuasca, there are many who consider that right throughout Amazonia they do not know of any shamans, only curanderos, facilitators of ayahuasca, or 'vegetalistas' (one who works with plants). Certainly, when the conditions are right, some of these curanderos, whether indigenous or western, do have the power to heal and possess what could be perceived magical powers. Yet, my other perception is that these men (they are mostly men) often do become exclusively driven by the profane trifecta of money, sex, and power. We must remember that shamanism in any culture is not a religion with a clear and singular view of the spiritual life. Many of the mestizo shamans actually contain Catholic elements in their practice. The truly indigenous master shamans of decades ago who lived deep within the jungle, are almost extinct, and since the 1950s or so, their presence is almost entirely absent. Also, it is useful to keep in mind that most of the shamanism that occurs in Amazonia is practised by those of 'mestizo' or mixed blood, and not a pure tribal tradition passed down from father to son. That kind of truly indigenous shamanism contains stories of how the world was created, and normally appears entirely un-sophisticated to Western people. Many of the most well known shamans who give ayahuasca to tourists are actually self-taught. The Shipibo tribe from Amazonian Peru do not teach 'shamanism' from teacher to student, as the most teaching is deemed to occur when communicating with the plants.

So when it comes to giving ayahuasca to gringos, the gringos want and desire a certain 'authenticity', and they are usually seeking visions. Yet, aya-huasca is often doing the deepest healing work when there are no visions occurring. The shaman may want you to become dependent on him and will offer you his brew and give you 'protection'. When smoking DMT or changa, you do not need a shaman. No ritual is strictly required. You smoke the DMT and are in the space for a short time and come back out of it. It is a raw and naked experience. You need to let go into the agency of the pres-ent. You don't need a shaman to protect you when you smoke DMT. The important thing is to let go into what you are experiencing. You can meet gnarly stuff out there too, but the universe is not purely chaotic; everything we are experiencing exists for a reason, and it is generally within our power to appropriately deal with whatever we are experiencing.

When it comes to ritual, I find the very act of drinking ayahuasca is the ritual or ceremony. The definition of a ceremony often implies solemnity and over-formality. That we are taking ourselves seriously does not mean we must perform token and symbolic motions. In my view, human ceremo-nies can be conducted informally, without pomp and pageantry, because the plants themselves do not typically present themselves with pomp and pageantry. I find the plants communicate in a rather personal and creative way. Then we can place ourselves in a framework where we can listen to the plants and possibly give ourselves the space to engage with one another. Someone once said to me, "wouldn't that just devolve into some sort of orgy?" Well, I've never experienced such a thing, but I guess that possibility is there. I find that if you give people permission to let go and possibly become crazy, it does tend to work a bit like reverse psychology. A part of their psyche is confronted by that freedom and instead of becoming crazy, they normally find their own centre, sanity, and their own way. Whereas, if you place rules and restrictions upon people, they will tend to be self-conscious and try to break those rules.

It is only the human psyche and its conditioning that wants to make a simple process a complex one. There is actually nothing to drinking ayahuasca – you drink a cup of a brew and experience its effects. People are often insecure and want a mental or egoic foundation, rather than to do the work to ascertain their own essential a priori foundation, which is more challenging. Religion or all these certain structures of thinking seem to be an archaic response to ontological uncertainty, which human beings find very confronting. It is easy to take up the religious ritual that the tribe recognises as being important. Not to take up any ritual or formulaic action is to face the self nakedly, which is much more challenging, and I think builds a much more flexible and stronger sort of character.

In the framework of Amazonian shamanism, while facilitating the drinking of ayahuasca, the shaman will generally be singing icaros, which call in certain plant spirits and beings to heal the body and process the energies of the group. These icaros are, of course, very effective and there is often an amplification of the effects the shaman is bringing into the space. In the framework of Santo Daime (essentially a church service in which ayahuasca is served as the sacrament) hymns are sung about the Virgin Mary, the rainforest, and Jesus (who are in some ways synonymous). The participants then dance the same dance and sing the same song, which is of course, the elements of religion condensed. In this way, Santo Daime people talk about being able to reach profound states of psychic and spiritual unity with one another. Yet, it is my belief that this potential for unity is innate in us, just as it is for the flocks of birds that fly in intuitive unison, or fish that swim in large schools in absolute synchronicity.

When the shaman is singing his songs, in a sense, you are witnessing a performance – often a brilliant performance, but still a performance. In this way, this format does not offer the participants the degree of unity they could experience. Yet, if the brew is strong enough, none of this even really matters, as you will be so far beyond anything that is occurring in the external world anyway.

In the sessions I conduct, I try and encourage a pregnant space where we are all given the space to tune into ourselves. Three years before I started facilitating ayahuasca sessions, I held a small group session where I blind-folded the participants so that they could not see each other until I took them into the room. Then I sat them in a circle and asked them to speak. In this way, I felt something new could come through that was not within society's sanctioned methods and means of communication. This is not to say that I feel an ayahuasca group should be about communication, com-munion, or any kind of group interaction – but perhaps we might want give those communications space to occur if they want to.

Essentially, the reason why ayahuasca groups exist is very simple. Ayahuas-ca is the medicine which the curandero may grow and/or knows how to prepare. Traditionally, Amazonian people go to them for physical healing, not to entertain the existence of other worlds and to see spirits, as these realities are normally taken for granted. It is also that dealing with these 'spiritual' things is the role which is given to the shaman. Yet, the word shaman is a new import into Amazonia. 'Vegetalista' is the traditional word used for one who is proficient in understanding the uses and properties of plants. Typically, ayahuasca is used to activate or open the channels to communicate with different plants and to more effectively perform heal-ing or various forms of sorcery. There are no ayahuasca dealers, and the curandero is not likely to give ayahuasca to people to take home, because they have normally come for healing.

The kind of reconnection to spirit many Westerners are commonly look-ing for is not guaranteed by the use of ayahuasca. It can help us make that reconnection, but it will not do it for us. Neither will iboga or any other psychoactive plant medicine. I would suggest a syncretic approach is necessary for those who wish to truly heal and reconnect with themselves. There are so many techniques and practices that Westerners have developed for each other, especially in the last few decades, that can help. But the inner work is present as itself for each individual; and each person has a different personal story and life potential to understand and fulfil.

Coming back into a reconnection with the self is the very essence of healing. Also, I personally feel a radical reappraisal of the very way we operate, relate, and live with each other is necessary – and this approach is often absent in the typical frameworks of the New Age. Through awareness and intelligence we can cultivate awareness and intelligence, and this is fundamental. Techniques, systems and even plants such as ayahuasca are not a necessary part of the curriculum for all. Life itself generally brings experiences and data to bear, which allows individuals to see what they need to face and what they have to deal with in their life. It is in the field of life we are directed to be present to, and the most essential data we receive will not typically come from buildings, books, computer games, furniture, plants, or animals, but from other people.

Thoughts on the Global Dance Party Scene

A few years into seriously taking psychedelics, I started taking them at outdoor forest parties. Up until that time, I had to train myself to take LSD at parties, as I did not find it at all easy being vulnerable among the different energies and intentions of all those people in such an exposed environment. It took me about half a dozen excursions until I became comfortable being at a party among other people on a psychedelic compound.

It was some years before I felt I could 'work' with the psychedelic space at 'doof' parties in the forest. That meant dancing, relating to what was present in people, and working through and processing what I felt to be present. Taking psychedelics at parties and trancing out and reaching a shamanic state of consciousness is perhaps almost a lost art. The intention of the pioneers in early 1990s Goa was to take a psychedelic, dance all night, and reach a deeply spiritual state of being. Sometime in the late 1990s, the music became less psychedelic, and hedonism, ego, and a much heavier, darker sound largely took over the global scene, except for rare pockets such as Finland and perhaps the rainforests of the far north coast of New South Wales, Australia.

There can be a great deal of value in dancing all night at such parties, as a good forest party can be akin to a religious experience. The first time I encountered the forest party scene in Finland was the closest to shamanism in the dance party scene that I had yet encountered. The DJ was looking at all the participants, noticing shifts in their energy; people would throw up from too much drinking (as Finnish people love to drink heavily) and the crowd would cheer, as people recognised this vomiting as a purge of the energy of the group. I later related excitedly to my newfound Finnish friends that I had only encountered such purging and understanding of its nature in ayahuasca sessions. I experienced the Finnish group dynamic of the dance floor to be quite a special unity, a dynamic moving whole. In comparison, I had never been quite as moved by any ayahuasca session I had participated in. In fact, when I danced and felt that synchronicity (something I had felt in Australia, but never as deeply as in Finland), astral tears came to my eyes. And when the outfit 'Luomohappo' finished playing their music inspired by traditional folk songs, I went into the forest and cried for 10 minutes, so touched was I with the tender and pure space of forest magic sustained by the Finnish forest party crew.

A shamanically oriented DJ, such as Franny from the far north coast of NSW in Australia, would often play very psychedelic music in contact and in tune with the energies of the dance floor and the crowd. In such an environment, someone such as myself is trying to really let the body go into dance, and many people report a peak experience which they describe as being danced, rather than dancing. In consciously engaging with the dance, circuits in the body open up, and more creativity and openness can occur in the dance. This is a good way to experience the body, to exercise the body, and to become more embodied and present. Psychedelics are not necessary for this kind of process to occur; but say 100 micrograms of good quality LSD does tend to facilitate letting go in dancing.

However, this space where individuals are supposed to be reaching a higher space by themselves, perhaps represents a kind of disassociated narcissism, in which people do not commonly dance with each other or interact. This form is thus, perhaps, the essence of New Age Transpersonalism. Interaction can happen for sure, but it is not the norm because transcendence, or a 'trance' state is presumably sought. Right from the beginning of the development of the electronic dance music scene, in the days of early techno, friends mentioned they never felt so lonely being at one of these parties, which makes sense, as this kind of alternative culture is very clearly the spawn of the highly individualised culture of the West.

I too have felt a sense of coldness in these disassociated and hyper-individuated cultures of gathering. The ideal of being interconnected and yet individualised has value for individuals and yet, relating is often absent. In the olden days, men and women always danced with each other at parties; however, the psychedelic trance world does not encourage 'the dance' of male and female and can at least tokenly represent a kind of non-sexualised space, different from nightclubs where the space is typically more overtly sexualised.

My sense is that the evolution of such spaces of human gathering will require social interaction, the space of dancing together, and the provision for a telepathic sensibility that transcends regular social sensibilities. There is always the potential for much more interaction that does not entirely rely on language – whereby people dance with one another, relating through dance, through energy and non-verbal contact, and these elements could represent a more evolved form of the electronic dance party phenomenon. In many respects, at a good party these elements are expressed to varying degrees. Yet, there is something about the dance between men and women that brings out the best in both participants, and the dance of Shiva/Shakti could be considered to be the primary dance. Small groups of friends do reach such spaces, but in larger spaces, where a more intimate dialogue of the body with other bodies on the dance floor could be achieved, would represent something of an evolution of that space.

People who attend 'electronic dance parties' are somewhat marginalised in most cultures. The form of outdoor dance parties is one of the most available forms of social gathering; anyone can attend, anyone can be accepted, so class-based societies do not typically respect that. Hierarchy does not exist on the surface, and yet, paradoxically, even in such spaces that are supposed to be free of hierarchy and the chimpanzee pecking order, social orders and hierarchy still very clearly exist. This sort of scene may consider itself above the Babylonian machinations of sex, money, and power, yet so often tends to be exactly about those machinations.

The psychedelic trance scene, like most subcultures, typically wears a more strict uniform than even mainstream cultures, where very clear and certain subcultural codes, in the form of clothing, language, and attitudes prevail. Even though the individual is promised individuation, at the end of the day the tribal codes prevail, and fitting in and conforming to those tribal codes is de rigueur if you want to be part of the tribe, which often considers itself 'special' and 'different' from other mere mortals who typically listen to less-driven and less-tribal electronic dance music.

Chapter Ten

Challenges and Meanings

The Challenges and Meanings of Drugs

There is clearly no sense in punishing and criminalising people for taking illicit drugs such as ice, cocaine, and cannabis. Although the usage of these drugs may represent 'recreational' and even 'social' use, many people are using these drugs as an avenue of escape, and many more are taking them because they are bored or unsatisfied with their lives. Others again are subject to some kind of suffering, acknowledged or unacknowledged, which the drugs are suppressing or repressing. All these motivations and reasons for taking 'drugs' are commonly combined for many people, and so it is rarely ever just one element that is driving most people's use of recreational drugs. Escapist drug use can sometimes seem to offend 'polite' society, in that it shows that individuals want to escape, demonstrating that boredom and suffering exists in what are often called 'normal' people. Many users of 'ice' or cocaine in Western countries are wealthy individuals, who may feel as if the use of these compounds serves as some sort of reward for their toils. The drugs may even assists them to carry out their toils in what is often a lifestyle of work addiction. However, the experiences brought about by such drugs are well known to be quite shallow and not inherently rich, fulfilling, or rewarding – and obviously, users will normally pay a price in terms of their health and well-being.

The root cause of 'drug abuse', I believe, is that Western society and culture is not nourishing in and of itself; the system/marketplace/government/

society and more obviously, the people who operate in Western society generally do not operate in order to nourish and provide for each other in this highly systemised and individualised culture. People then seek nourishment in drugs, but rarely do they find it, and our monkey claw reaches out for something that will give us that instant boost or 'hit' not often found in our everyday lives. We are often hungry for something to happen to us internally or externally, but at the end of the day, it is us who make things happen through our own endeavours and efforts.

Our society exists in an unfortunate circumstance, when it is so often that the masses turn to drugs to alleviate the lack of fulfilment in their lives, working long hours, and not receiving much of a reward except more work hours and daily stress. Under these circumstances of 'wage slavery', it is easy to understand why so many people use drugs – and especially why so many people smoke cigarettes and drink so much alcohol. Drugs are clearly a societal issue, and in a society where monetary and material values are typically given priority over human values, the fault lies with society and the regressive views that many individuals continue to maintain in regard to 'drugs'. Another problem is the lack of true healing work carried out by individuals in society, which can address the primary and core issues causing suffering and boredom. In the West, we typically pursue happiness in the marketplace, but how many people are actually happy? The enormous number of people taking anti-depressants in Western countries is a clear and obvious indicator of the lack of authentic happiness in such countries. Therefore criminalising drugs is not the most successful harm-minimisation strategy or solution to the 'drug abuse' problem, because the underlying reasons and issues leading to people using drugs are not being humanly addressed.

Punishing drug users without dealing with or acknowledging the root-cause of such use is indicative of an immature society. A mature society would give people responsibility to find out what is best for them, and offer guidance which promotes mature and conscious use. If cocaine was cheap, legal and plentiful, what societal problems would this create? If you could purchase high quality heroin legally, would you do it? I personally don't like heroin very much, but I would much rather inject high-quality heroin than get seriously drunk. There are also times in life where turmoil and suffering do exist. I am not saying that we should necessarily turn to drugs to alleviate our suffering, but for many, comfort can be found in ice cream or chocolate, while for others, marijuana alleviates stress. Furthermore, many people already use legal drugs such as benzos and anti-depressants to alleviate stress, and it may actually be the case that some drugs that today are illegal would better help these people.

In countries that clamp down hard on people for using drugs, such as Sweden or the United States, you will often find quite an immature 'drug culture'. In cultures where people can explore, evolve, and create a mature and informed drug culture, people seem to be much more intelligently self-regulating than governments would typically give them credit for. In an ailing culture, people will continually be turning to 'drugs' for some kind of substance they are not getting in their lives. Even then, that substance is not ultimately real or very fulfilling. Cigarette smokers will commonly tell you that, without smoking tobacco, they become bored and perhaps that it is one of their pleasures in life. But really, how exciting is smoking tobacco? Most people in Western countries have a childish relationship to substances, that can be summed up in the saying 'you only want what you can't have'. Therefore, we make substances like cocaine into a 'bad big deal'. If cocaine were readily available and cheap, many would take it all day and every day. Yet, a lot of people wouldn't take it at all. Many would take it a lot at first and then cut down their usage to find out what works best for their body and system. For most people I know, myself included, cocaine only really works as a basic stimulant, even when the dosage is dramatically increased.

It is clear to many that decriminalisation is the only sane way forward, because at the very least, prohibition supports and allows a dark criminal underworld to thrive. How would this criminal underworld even exist to the same degree that it does now, without drugs? Perhaps the criminals would revert back to the good old days of 'protection rackets'? Corporations and government agencies in many countries of the world are quite commonly in cahoots with gangsters and cartels that like to keep drug prices high. This kind of corruption is clearly the biggest political problem that must be overcome before the enormous amount of suffering caused by the illicit drug trade can be ameliorated. If we decriminalised all drugs and made them available in specialist shops where people knew about them, and recommendations could be given about their use and potential misuse, we would be on the way to creating a mature culture. We would then also experience a new set of potential problems, but also necessary challenges.

A primary issue in the current culture of prohibition is that the people who could be taking the most from experiences with psychedelics are typically not accessing them. In a more enlightened culture, couples could explore the use of MDMA for working through issues in their relationship, people's depression could be treated with ketamine, and heroin addicts could be openly treated with iboga or ibogaine. Such a change in legal policy has the potential to open up many service industries. Indigenous peoples would be more able to share their sacred entheogenic plants and knowledge to potential initiates from all over the world, rather than a small number of tribal initiates. Bringing these materials into the same economy as other goods could only work favorably in the end. In an apparently economically squeezed world, one good way to instantly increase revenue would be to tax these substances. Then we can admit the use of these compounds and further our understanding of the human psyche and mind in relation to them. Perhaps most importantly, we could then attempt to develop a mature culture, where further research into psychoactive plants and compounds could be funded and the bio-chemical nature of the human psyche more deeply explored and understood.

If governments were to tax these substances, any cost that may be incurred from a presumed increase in consumption of presumably dangerous drugs could easily be recouped, and the remainder spent on sensible, conscious and human government policy. For many people, the allure and interest to take 'drugs' would be lost, and drug quality could increase. Many of the damaging health effects that illicit drugs have is because they are made without care and concern, from crude chemicals and with many potentially harmful additives. None of these ideas are at all new and have been espoused by many esteemed people for a very long time. The revolution will likely occur within small countries taking the opportunity to change the laws in their country despite various political forces, in order to improve their economy and provide the people with a sane public policy. Such a policy would not hurt the country, economically or socially, by putting its citizens in jail for victimless 'crimes'.

The Drugs Don't Work

Perhaps recreational drugs are an offensive idea for many because they appear to represent an escape from present circumstances and imply an inclination to not deal with life as it is. Neither do most approaches to taking drugs truly work for dealing with or not dealing with one's life. As The Verve's song goes: "the drugs don't work, they just make you worse." And drugs often don't continue to really work because of the effect of tolerance. At the end of the day, there is something unsatisfactory with the typical states produced by many compounds. It is like sex without connection, which is then only a mechanical, biological process. The ever so common nihilism of the Western psyche provides for non-connectiveness quite easily, but the point is, sex is ultimately an expression of relationship, the essential meaning of which the body will quite simply define for us. For many, sex is 'meaningless', and they don't really enjoy it beyond the idea of its occurrence, because there is no provision given to sex as any form of relationship or relating. Then, all we are left with is an act of biological functionality and the ideology of pleasure and egoic validation.

For many people, MDMA is going to be the strongest 'heart opening' they have ever experienced, partly because the body is brought to realise and release its defences when their personal armour loosens and their guard comes down. The first time you take MDMA is always by far the best, because the system is then completely 'tricked', and the second or third time is nowhere near as good – and this pattern remains the same for many substances. Many compounds, such as the MDMA-like methylone or 4-FMP, commonly stop working altogether after you take them a half a dozen or so times, as the brain will then flat out refuse to be tricked. Perhaps the most meaningful phenomenon of psychotropic drugs is how they can influence the perceived non-physical, as much or more through the biofeedback system of body/mind/soma/spirit than through pure 'effect'. The mystery of psychedelics is that they appear to show us something of the intersection of matter and spirit. Spirit is meaning, yet matter is not meaningless or necessarily apart from the spiritual, as Cartesian dualism would have us assume. Matter can be perceived as a means through which we can focus upon the nature of life. When the ayahuasca or iboga spirit engages with our physical selves, it *chooses* to engage. It is quite common that people will take iboga, salvia or ayahuasca vine and nothing will happen, as the plant spirit has chosen not to appear and relate.

As much as many like the idea of instant pleasure from a substance, for most, it never quite truly ticks the boxes as to what accounts for real plea-sure and fulfilment. The insanity of addiction is that we never quite get what we need from what we desire, but never see a way to get what we need apart from the substance, which doesn't really give us what we need! People often say you should be able to get high without substances, as if getting 'high' was the point or an end in and of itself. In my experience and from the reports of many others, the human psyche can take us to many different places that go far beyond being 'high', but most people are not aligned to a path that is going to get them that 'high' on their own. Human fulfilment goes far beyond brain chemicals, it is about living in such a way that we are plugged in and aware, choosing to be receptive and proactive, being fulfilled by our own motions in life. I think many forget it is normally only when we are in the company of other human beings that we are triggered or moved, and experience the most essential depths of ourselves.

When we take the attitude that the chemical is all we need, then we are missing out on a potential communion with the plant spirit. Purified ibogaine is perceived by many to be somewhat less efficacious than iboga root bark or a total alkaloidal extract of the root bark. To take that purified ibogaine is analogous to purifying the mescaline alkaloid from peyote and forsaking half of the other few dozen magical alkaloids in peyote. In my experience, purified cocaine does not normally compare to chewing five grams of dried coca leaf. There is a certain apparent power in the purified compound because it is no longer embedded within a natural basis of other alkaloids and co-factors that buffer its action into a comprehensible texture. That is not to say there is no connection to the plant spirit when people take purified cocaine. But when chewing coca leaves, there is liter-ally a certain heart-opening effect that is simply not obtainable with purified cocaine. Yet, high quality, well-made cocaine, even though it is almost impossibly rare, can be effective as a true medicine. Similarly, pure glassy crystal DMT extracted from acacia trees is very effective, and many DMT smokers prefer its clarity and cerebral nature. But most of the old-timers in Australia and Europe prefer the DMT that looks more opaque and can be quite waxy and oily, and that is because these extracts contain other magical and potent alkaloids, many of which are still presently unknown and unnamed.

Credible Futures

Simply put, we give 'drugs' too much credibility by making them illegal and making them out to be such a big deal. Cocaine is not a path to ecstasy; neither is heroin or meth. The highest high I ever had on extremely potent intravenous crystal meth doesn't compare to meaningful moments with a loved one and I've never personally felt much 'love' via MDMA. Love has simply appeared when it has, and there is an immense richness in that. States that MDMA can catalyse are often relatively noisy and can be hard on the body. I have also found that while MDMA taken with lovers can facilitate connection, it can also just as often prevent real connection and authentic opening.

At the end of the day, most 'street' drugs are somewhat superficial, just as we consider coffee to be superficial, or at least not a big deal – you have a cup with your breakfast. In Peru, coca tea containing cocaine is widely available as a healthy hot drink. Puritanical North American society often likes to posit drugs as a 'bad' big deal, and perhaps this collectively enforced view of drugs operates as a form of reverse psychology. Nowhere else in the world do people have such an apparent need for drugs. Nowhere in the world are so many people punished so severely for taking drugs, and nowhere in the world do so many people make so much money from drugs.

In my observation and experience, alcohol is one of the most dangerous drugs. I have never had dreams telling me to stop taking particular substances, but I had a dream the night I got really drunk one Christmas that showed me the forest of my brain to have been like burnt out charcoal after a forest fire had raged through my inner terrain. Very clearly, alcohol reigns as the drug of choice in Western society, as it allows the release of social inhibitions and encourages the sexes to more easily meet and mingle. This is not necessarily problematic in and of itself, but the utilisation of the drug alcohol is clearly not the most integrated or intelligent way to socially interact with the opposite sex. That is not to say that there are no health problems in the ingestion of different sorts of substances that are now largely illicit, but friends and I have noticed quite outrageously negative effects even from drinking coffee. I find a line of good cocaine more useful than coffee as a stimulant, and it seems to have a less stressful effect on my body than most coffee. Taking cocaine, even a few times a day, doesn't give me the jitters or keep me awake at night or 'give me the shits' like drinking a few cups of strong coffee a day will.

Heroin is normally considered the most 'bad' and 'dangerous' drug. Perhaps, it is the idea of potentially getting 'hooked' and becoming a heroin user that fascinates people. After taking heroin intravenously over a dozen times spaced out over many years, I never really saw the appeal. People are scared of being 'hooked', but it takes sincere effort to become addicted to heroin. Many people I know agree – heroin is just not that great. And that is the point, for most people's body chemistry there is no drug that is that great simply because the drug is forcing the body to produce an effect, and the body's own reward systems are more powerful than physical compounds. Often it seems that the 'drug user' is socially castigated because they do not affirm their own reward system and have instead replaced that with an inferior system that typically doesn't even really work.

When I talk about certain experiences I have had, such people cannot understand that I wasn't intoxicated at the time. I have given psychedelics to diagnosed 'schizophrenics', who were never very impressed by their effects, and it is clear to me that the brain can create much more immersive psychoactive states than most substances can provide. When I took 1000 micrograms of LSD in the Kimberley, Australia (one of the most remote and naturally intact places on the planet), I realised very clearly that the LSD was operating as a kind of noise that prevented me from truly experiencing the wonder of the nature there. Other times in sacred sites in the Kimberley, when I woke up at 5 am in the morning, completely free of social and cultural noise pollution, were just as potent as taking 1000 micrograms of LSD. Actually, taking 1000 micrograms in that environment did not particularly plug me into a different sort of experience. In such a place (and such places exist in most parts of the world), nature can transport you into an altered state. Being in such a place is part of a recipe for meaningful experiences. Rather than relying on substances to produce meaning, it is more useful to rely on ourselves to generate meaningful experiences.

My ever so obvious conclusion is this: people compulsively take street drugs because they are unhappy, unsatisfied, or bored. Human beings are not inherently dysfunctional, but Western society and its values makes them so. Because in Western society, people are put below abstract values in the guise of over-survival of the fittest, which is clearly dysfunctional. The ego can choose to buffer this dysfunctionality and resulting inner void by taking 'drugs', or it can be faced head on, and true healing, individual and collective, can then occur. Psychoactive plants can especially help to guide, catalyse and heal, but it does benefit individuals to rely on such psychoactive plants for coming to terms with themselves, as the inner and outer work that each of us needs to face, is simply present.

A conscious and mature approach to psychedelics involves focusing upon our capacity to create meaning in our lives and to release and remove what prevents such meaning and realisation from occurring through the self-awareness facilitated by the psychedelic compound. The many layers and levels of an individual's possible realisation are immense, and what each of us is called to understand and work through is entirely unique.

Appendix I

Changa:
Smoking DMT infused into
Ayahuasca and other Herbs

Changa is the colloquial name I gave to a smoking mix containing naturally sourced DMT, *Banisteriopsis caapi* and various herbs that have a synergistic effect when blended together. Very simply, changa allows people to smoke DMT more easily and to get more from their DMT smoking experience. 'Dreamleaf' or just 'Dreamtime' are perhaps more formal names that have been given to this material. Yet changa (chang-ah) is very definitely the proper Australian slang name for this blend, which may make some Australians wince and/or smile, and people from other countries to raise an eyebrow or two!

In order to make changa, DMT is simply infused into a blend of herbs that is easily dissolved into alcohol or any form of ethanol. Although it is true that a few people here and there have been dissolving DMT into herbs for many decades, it is the combination of the DMT with ayahuasca vine and the intelligent alchemy of this combination of herbs, similar to an ayahuasca brew, that gives changa its unique nature and power. My preferred method for making changa is to melt the DMT on a plate or tray over a steam bath, then adding a few dozen millilitres of high quality vodka into which the DMT dissolves. The herbs are then added to the tray or the plate and stirred extremely well. The herbs then dry quite quickly, whereas dissolving the DMT into cold ethanol or acetone, and then mixing the herbs, tends to take more time to dry. However, the result is basically the same.

A basic and standard ratio for much of the gentler changa that many people make is around 25% DMT content by weight. So, in one gram of changa at this strength, there is 250 mg of DMT; and within four grams of changa, there is one gram of DMT. This equates to 30 light experiences, 20 pretty decent experiences, 10 much stronger experiences and 5 very strong experiences. However, a 30% blend is stronger, with the 40-50% DMT blends being very strong and equating to, or even exceeding, the strength of smoking freebase DMT by itself. This initial standard ratio of 25 % DMT changa was never designed to provide a fully immersive 'out of body' hyperspatial experience. Although, as most people who work with DMT know, sometimes it only takes a little to really take you there. The high dose breakthrough DMT experience is something that many people may only want to visit once or a few times in their life. DMT is normally so strong, so intense, that more is often less.

With 20-30% changa, people can access DMT comfortably in a way that is likely to be beneficial, but not requiring days or years to process the experience. However, for a fully immersive DMT experience, most people generally need to freebase from 50mg to even as much as 150 mg DMT and most people find these sorts of amounts difficult to smoke in a freebase pipe. For that breakthough experience via 20-30 % changa, I would recommend people either quickly smoke two to three successive bong or pipe hits or just take one big pipe. It just depends on how much changa people use in their pipe cone and how refined or coarse the herbs are. With 40-50% DMT changa (there is no reason to go beyond 50% in my opinion), it should only take one good bong or pipe hit to really engage into breakthrough states where dying of astonishment at the nature of the inexpressible is the order of the day.

I generally recommend smoking pure DMT through a water bong and then wedging the amount of DMT you want to smoke between a layer of passionflower and/or finely shredded ayahuasca vine, so that the lighter flame does not make direct contact with the DMT. This is called 'the sandwich method'. Then you should simply smoke all the herbs in one hit. The efficaciousness of the DMT is quite often dependent on getting the most DMT to the system in the shortest amount of time. That being said, in light of the existence of changa, many are tending to feel that smoked crystal DMT by itself is too disconnected, cerebral, 'alien', shortlived and difficult to remember. Whereas, the changa experience is often more integrated, connected and relevant to the human form. This is because the ayahuasca and other herbs assist the DMT to be most relevant to the human system.

Many people around the world are beginning to smoke changa through a pipe device called a 'vaporgenie'. This pipe is a simple and inexpensive way to vaporise smoking herbs in a small, regular looking pipe. The result is a smoother smoke, that some say is 'the best way' to smoke changa. However, myself and many others prefer the immediacy of smoking the herbs, rather than vaporising them. However, many people do prefer to use a vapourgenie or mechanical hand held vapouriser simply because it is much easier to smoke DMT this way.

The primary herb to be used in changa is *Banisteriopsis caapi*, which should consist of at least 25% of the herbs used in order to be truly effective. Both leaf and vine from the plant can be used, with leaf providing a smoother, cerebral smoke, and the vine itself providing an earthier, often more potent effect. The theory behind using caapi in changa, is that you are making something of a smokable ayahuasca brew, combining the vine, the DMT and other admixture plants into the whole works to provide a synergistic effect. The admixture plants in ayahuasca brews are typically activated by the presence of the caapi, as by themselves they are not nearly as potent.

I figure that any herb used in changa has its potency increased by a factor of ten. So the herb mullein (a potent lung herb normally drunk as a tea), when smoked in a changa blend, has the potential to give the most fantastic and instantaneous lung healings. This sort of healing has traditionally only been possible with ayahuasca brews.

When available, I prefer combining ayahuasca leaf and vine in various ratios. It is important to shred the vine finely enough so that it burns properly, although powdered vine may often be too fine when combined with other herbs. Good vine will provide a nice afterglow when the experience has worn off, whereas vine leaf will not normally provide this. Cielo or yellow ayahuasca vine is recommended, although any type of caapi will work fine, as long as it is over three to four years old and thicker than a human's thumb.

The basic theory behind changa is that very small amounts of smoked harmine, even 100 micrograms to 1mg, can effect as much as a 50% MAO-A inhibition and beyond. Furthermore, it is known that caapi extract is 100 to 1000 fold more potent than isolated harmine as an MAO-A inhibitor. (Schwarz et al. 2003) This is why when you use 300mg of vine or leaf in 1g of changa, it can still have a potent effect, not something that many people understand. Because they still think they must always boost the harmine content of changa in order for it to be effective. But if your vine is 1% harmine, 300mg of vine would contain 3mg of harmine. Say if there is 15 medium smoking experience in 1 gram of changa, this means that 200mcg is in each smoke, plenty enough to effect more than 50% MAO-A inhibition. Even using 300mg of vine per gram of changa, you can still get 30-40 minute experiences at times. Much of it also depends on the strength of your vine in the first place as well, which of course can vary greatly. This MAO-A inhibition appears to occur as instantaneously, as say, the effects of smoking freebase recreational drugs, such as cocaine or methamphetamine. This MAO-A inhibition enables what previously would be a 5 to 10 minute experience to become more like an 10 to 20 minute experience, or even an experience lasting half an hour to an hour.

Changa has been commonly reported to consist of simply *Banisteriopsis caapi* leaf and DMT, and this recipe works very well and can have a very smooth quality to it, but this blend, I think, tends to lack the colourful alchemy and flavour of the other admixture herbs. Any herb or plant can be used in changa, and many different herbs are being used by different people around the world in different ratios and blends. It should be kept in mind that the ayahuasca element activates the herbs used, and each new herb may not have the desired effect, or may have an unpredictable effect. As an example, we have noticed that the addition of skullcap at 20 percent of the herbs used tends to put people to sleep immediately after smoking changa!

So, a 'classic' and 'original' changa blend that has stood the test of time looks something like this:

- 30% ayahuasca vine and/or leaf
- 20% mullein
- 20% passionflower
- 20% peppermint
- 5% calendula
- 5% blue lotus

Both calendula and blue lotus must be added after combining the DMT in order to preserve their colour and texture. Mullein can also be substituted with coltsfoot, another powerful lung herb that tends to have more of an expectorant quality. This can be good for people's lungs, but can also become a bit snotty and noisy for many people. In general, I prefer mullein because of its fluffy consistency and more benign effect. The passionflower provides another MAOI imprint as well as a nice calming, sedative effect, which counteracts and balances out the awakening and brightening effect of DMT. The peppermint is added to smooth out the smoke and give the blend a more pleasant taste. In fact, a good blend should be like not smoking anything at all – it is that transparent. Calendula or marigold is a classic nurturing and all-round healing flower, and is added for the quality of its vibrational support. Blue lotus or lily (or any other psychoactive lilies or lotuses) gives the blend a 'top note' and also adds a smoother taste, and can be used to up to about 20% of the mixture. Damiana is another herb that can be used, adding a pleasant warmth and euphoria to the blend. When available, *Justicia pectoralis* is very nice in changa and is effective at around 10 percent of the herbal content. Justicia seems to have a balancing and smoothing effect upon the body's utilisation of tryptamines, and its flowers are traditionally added to tryptamine snuffs used in the Amazon.

All the herbs should be 'groomed', so that all sticks and inconsistent stems are removed. A coffee grinder can be used on 'burst' setting to ensure that the herbs are consistently sized. Some prefer a very fine blend so that more can be smoked in a cone, whereas some prefer a more full-bodied blend with larger herbal bits and pieces.

Some have reported that small amounts of *Salvia divinorum* leaf in a changa blend brings out the best of this plant. However, I feel this plant is best left to people's individual relationship, rather than adding it to a blend that many may partake of, as salvia can tend to take over, with people having full scale salvia experiences, rather than anything like a changa experience. I would say the same regarding the addition of cannabis, which many do not want to partake of. Some people have been adding small amounts of brugmansia or datura flowers to their blend. Interestingly, this flower is added to the ayahuasca brews in the Amazon and is said to increase the visual aspect of the brew. Most curanderos would not even consider taking this plant on its own and consider the usage of this plant in brews as something one must be very careful with, because if you add too much, the effects can be variously undesirable, though not likely dangerously so.

I definitely think that synthetic 5-MeO-DMT should not be combined with MAOI's at any stage, and again, 5-MeO-DMT is quite strong enough by itself. I am yet to be convinced that any other research chemicals or additives in a changa-like blend are useful or better than natural DMT. However, a herbal blend I dubbed 'cracker', containing 5 to 10 percent 5-MeO-DMT, has been found to be a very effective way to dose and smoke 5-MeO-DMT, as it contains classic changa herbs such as mullein, mint and blue lotus. I have not found 5-MeO-DMT to be at all positively affected or enhanced by beta-carbolines from ayahuasca vine or Syrian rue and have personally had very negative experiences combining beta-carbolines with 5-MeO-DMT. The Erowid website has received several reports of people experiencing very troubling side effects with this combination, and there have even been a few reports of deaths when people take far too much 5-MeO-DMT with an MAOI. I personally think that Syrian rue is an unnecessary addition to changa and the seeds will be quite unpleasant to smoke. Friends have reported that the addition of a simple Manske extract of crystalline harmaline has additional benefits, but this may be too strong for many people, and I have never seen why this would be necessary. I have found that changa blends with added harmalas can be more scattered and less focused than those blends which contain extracted harmine from ayahuasca vine.

Harmine, and to a lesser degree tetrahydroharmine from the *Banisteriopsis caapi* vine, are the key alkaloids in changa which have a wondrous synergy with DMT in low doses. Friends have been reporting very pleasant effects, by soaking shredded vine and/or leaf in ethanol or alcohol and then making something like a 10X ayahuasca leaf blend with the alkaloids, say from 100 grams of leaf infused into 10 grams of leaf. Again, many find the resulting effect to be too strong or weighted towards heavy, overt body sensations. I personally think that a 2x blend is strong enough, and may be too strong for many. A 2x blend is where for example, you are using 300mg of vine in 1 gram of changa and use the extracted alkaloids (say via soaking the vine in ethanol) from another 300mg of vine infused to the blend. One friend has reported that making a 10x extract from Passionflower is however, a very pleasant and smooth smoke, as the harmine content in passionflower by itself is too weak to be noticeable.

In Australia, we can obtain DMT from many different acacia species, such as the two rather common Australian wattle trees species – *Acacia obtusifolia* and *Acacia acuminata*. *Acacia obtusifolia* is quite strong and visual in its effect and *Acacia acuminata* is often more gentle and relaxed. People from outside of Australia will generally use *Mimosa hostilis* root bark, although a friend said to me once quite cheekily that he thought using this DMT source in changa would be like 'kissing your sister'! Synthetic DMT could be used in changa, although most find naturally sourced DMT to be richer and have a smoother and more integrated imprint of a living organism, which tends to align with the human system and provide the most relevant informational interchange. Each source of DMT is entirely different, with different qualities and 'teachings' – simply because each plant species has a different spirit and communication. Don't take my word for it though. Try half a dozen DMT- containing species a dozen times each and then get back to me!

Changa makes DMT more accessible and available to people, it is not addictive (as DMT is not addictive) and it is largely safe. I have not heard of anyone running into any real trouble with it (whereas, inexperienced and normally uninformed people can sometimes terrify themselves by smoking too much pure DMT). Some people tend to keep reaching back for it, but most people tend to not pursue changa on a regular basis. I think changa is best smoked irregularly to get the most out of it. For some, changa remains purely recreational. Yet we find that, just with DMT, it will continue to take you deeper and deeper the more you smoke it. Some amount of respect is required to get the most out of DMT, which many learn in response to using it. My personal experience is that there is a limit to the number of times I can smoke changa in a row (usually about three or four times), and after that the experience tends to experientially degrade. This does not appear to be at all an issue of physical tolerance, as some people are able to keep smoking for many hours on end, without any lessening of effects. When smoking by oneself, it is good to sit up or lie down and just experience the state. When smoking with other people, it is best to be silent and just experience the state – although dancing or singing is highly appropriate behaviour.

For most people, the initial state will be an expanded state of awareness, similar to the state of LSD or any psychedelic. For many, the next step into the experience will consist of geometric patterns and colours. Others will have visual experiences that tend to be coherent and appear to arise from an 'alien' realm rather than being a mere projection of the individual body or mind. For some people, this may involve contact with entities not ordinarily visible to the human eye. These experiences tend to be highly vivid and possibly very transformative, representing one of the more liberating possibilities of smoking DMT. I believe that smoking DMT in this form is particularly beneficial to those from Western cultures, where the existence of other realms or planes of being is generally not considered 'real'. Changa does combine well with many common psychedelic substances such as LSD, and it can also help a weak ayahuasca brew 'kick in' (likely due to the MAOI's), although I would suggest people who rely on changa for a boost to their ayahuasca experience to simply increase the amount of DMT they are using in their brews.

The general effect of changa is normally quite healing, and the mind, body and psyche tend to become more integrated. DMT, as a meta-neurotransmitter, appears to allow the transmission and modulation of more information between neurons. The mind is stilled, the body quietens, and contact with the ineffable is often made. All this generally works to clear the mind, align the psyche, and fulfil the spirit. People are then able to get on with their lives with more perspective and perhaps more motivation.

It is quite common for people to give up decades-long addictions to substances such as crystal meth or cocaine after smoking changa for the first time. Other individual reports of benefits are quite varied and vast. Precautions related to the presumed toxic effects from taking an MAOI are generally overstated as a danger within the West. In some rare instances, people will report strange reactions and feeling ill from smoking changa with no known MAOI contraindications, and these reactions are as yet unexplainable. However, people who have taken MDMA or those who are taking an SSRI may wish to avoid changa, as there is the possibility of 'serotonin syndrome', which occurs when the body is overwhelmed by too much serotonin and in rare instances could be life threatening if not treated.

Smoking changa is probably no more or less detrimental than any other form of smoking, yet I would highlight this as a possible negative aspect which people should be aware of. That being said, DMT is a very powerful catalyst of change. Many people will have their eyes opened in a way they may not feel they have been prepared for. There is normally no way to go back to the previous way of viewing the world, once a new way of perceiving the world has become apparent. Changa can open people's eyes and allow them a special and novel experience – but it is over the few hours that ayahuasca or other DMT and MAOI preparations lasts where often the greatest amount of inner work can be carried out. That being said, a strong changa journey can take people into places that ayahuasca will not normally be able to. Smoked DMT will almost always result in a clearer and deeper experience than the peak of an ayahuasca journey. I think that this DMT preparation is indeed quite special, and represents a user-friendly medium that can allow access to the medicinal power of plant alchemy and visionary states of great personal value.

Appendix II

The Origin and Utilisation of Changa

Changa (chang-ah – typical Australian pronunciation or chan-gah – typical European or South American pronunciation) is best defined as a smoking mixture containing ayahuasca vine and/or leaf, and an intelligent combination of several admixture herbs and naturally sourced DMT that has been infused into these herbs.

In Australia during the very early noughties, in the shire of Byron Bay, there were only a few people extracting DMT from acacia species. At that time, the intensity of the DMT experience and the difficulty of smoking DMT crystal were intimidating to most people. A friend called 'The Cybermutant' and I initiated the smoked DMT crystal experience to hundreds of people in those years. During that time, we learnt a lot about how to make sure that people smoked DMT properly, how to support people to be in the most conducive mindset, how to ensure the best physical environment for them to journey deeply, how to be present to them in a space of witnessing, and also, after they had smoked the DMT, how to question and listen to their debriefing. We were always very impressed by the power of DMT to expand people's paradigm and create authentic awe regarding the awesomeness of life itself. Many said that the experience was life changing and a profound reference point for everything they did in their lives. Yet, DMT crystal in its raw state was tricky to use, and very few knew how to smoke it effectively, let alone obtain it in the first place. The 'breakthrough' experience that most tried to reach was so powerful that many of those initiated with crystal only wanted to take DMT that way once.

Changa first came to exist in late 2003. Around this time 'The Chocolate Beast' was extracting DMT from acacias and obtaining a high yield of 0.8% from the bark of an *Acacia Obtusifolia* tree, and yet through no technical fault of his own, the resulting material always came out as goo! The goo was perfectly good to smoke, but how to get anyone to smoke it? It was almost impossible to transport, it got on your hands easily and continually had to be scraped off any given surface.

I had read in Jonathan Ott's book *Pharmacotheon: Entheogenic Drugs, Their Plant Sources and History*, that in 1970's USA people would infuse DMT into herbs, especially parsley, at a ratio of 10%, which seemed like a very small concentration of DMT to me. Later tests would reveal this is an especially weak smoking mix. An online correspondent in Europe told me that he also infused DMT into parsley for smoking DMT at times, but nowhere in Australia had I ever come across DMT infused into herbs and neither had anyone I knew.

For a couple of years, I had been giving people *Banisteriopsis caapi* (ayahuasca) vine shavings to smoke. Some quite prominent people around Byron Bay, Australia, said they felt aligned and balanced out all day from smoking ayahuasca vine by itself. Quite regularly, we were smoking 100 mg of DMT sprinkled onto an ayahuasca vine joint, which we called a luxury joint, and this would be passed around at parties or among ourselves. After passing around the joint, we would then dance and sing or just sit in silence. So it seemed like a good idea to try and infuse this goo into the shredded ayahuasca vine at a ratio of 50%. Therefore, one gram of DMT was infused into every two grams of ayahuasca vine shavings. This mix was shared all over the Byron region for free to all who wanted it. People liked it, but a few said it was too strong, and even the most hard-core DMT smokers said it was too strong as a smoke and also as an experience.

Having heard from another researcher that smoking DMT with mullein (a lung herb) and peppermint was a very good way to smoke DMT, we mixed these herbs in with the ayahuasca vine, added passionflower for its harmine and relaxing qualities, as well as some blue lotus to give the mix some colour. We then reduced its ratio at first to 17.5%, which worked fine, and then up to 25%, or a ratio of 3 grams of herbs to 1 gram of DMT, which seemed to work best. Then began the testing – giving out this 'smoking mix' to people, and seeing what they thought of it. Sometimes that meant gathering little groups of people at parties and smoking it in a circle around a fire. All the responses were favourable: people liked it, because it was like DMT, but much more gentle than most people's experiences with crystal DMT. Reports came in of people smoking this mix and giving up decades old meth or coke addictions.

During an ayahuasca session I facilitated, I decided this smoking mix must have a name and the word that 'came through' or just simply arose in my mind was 'changa'. The word had a colloquial ring to it that appeared para-doxical and earthy, compared to the spacey and exotic nature of the places it could allow you to access. The good thing about changa is that it is a blend of herbs which appears much more friendly than DMT crystal. Anyone can simply put the herbs into their pipe or roll it up by itself, smoke it, and get something from it. The experiences induced from changa were sub-break-through experiences, not the typical breakthrough experiences that most associate with DMT crystal. With DMT crystal, you are typically either going to breakthrough or not, and there is often very little space between.

The basic theory of changa is that the admixture herbs included in the blend are activated/potentiated not only by the ayahuasca leaf and/or vine, but also by the DMT. I found that the addition of mullein, made the blend much easier to smoke. I experienced some incredible lung healings by smoking changa containing mullein, as at that time I was smoking ciga-rettes and my lungs often felt very out of shape. I figured that the DMT and the ayahuasca vine seemed to activate the qualities of the mullein in the same way as admixture plants used in the Amazon are primarily activated by the ayahuasca, but also to a degree by the DMT as well.

Even though changa is easier to smoke than freebase crystal DMT, I doubt there is anything in the world that is actually good for the lungs when you smoke it. DMT is known to be quite a harsh smoke, and I feel this is clearly the biggest drawback of changa. It is for this reason that it is probably best only smoked occasionally. Having said that, one hardcore cigarette and pot smoker told me that smoking DMT saved his lungs, and others have told me that they thought smoking DMT was good for their lungs!

I have had experiences where I have smoked a very large amount of crystal DMT and become unconscious. Coming to, I looked down at my hand which contained a big pile of black mucous. My friends said I had coughed and snorted in strange ways and spent five minutes coughing up all this mucous. We have also noticed when using coltsfoot in changa, rather than mullein, that people will quite commonly cough up mucus.

Changa unequivocally lasts longer than smoking DMT crystal, perhaps up to 40 minutes (normally more like 10-20 minutes). This is easy to test. Smoke the same amount of DMT as crystal and in changa. The changa experience will almost always be longer, smoother, more intricate, and have a pleasant afterglow. It works this way because harmine is very effective as an MAO inhibitor when smoked, with amounts of only 100 micrograms being able to effect 50 % MAO-A inhibition. The effects of the MAO inhibitor are as instantaneous as smoking DMT or compounds normally considered more nefarious! Yet, what is really happening here is that the ayahuasca spirit is engaging with the human organism and carrying out essential healing work on different layers of the bio-electrical system, which can often be clearly felt by those attuned to this experience. You simply will not have this same feeling when smoking DMT crystal – the experience will normally feel emptier and less integrated.

Changa allows people to smoke DMT at what we call a 'sub-breakthrough' level. In that case, one does not travel out of body or enter into another dimension. The point is that many people are told not to go into hyperspace. It is very common for people to be turned away and told they have already been shown 'all this', and so why are they coming back? At the first level, which can be very pleasant, there is just a feeling. There may be no visuals, but there is a heightening of the senses and visceral awareness. At the second level, there are visuals, whether they are geometric patterns or more sophisticated forms. Typically, this level represents a level of communion and communication with the spirit of the DMT-containing plant, which is the artist painting the visuals upon the inner vision of the person who has smoked the DMT. Beyond this level, there is contact with deeper, often extraordinary spiritual realities – or people may experience alien beings or earth spirits and perhaps, other 'paranormal or 'ultra normal' phenomena. Upon first smoking DMT there is often a barrier that one passes through, a kind of membrane, which can be a little bit intense. But over time, the experience becomes smoother and smoother, until one is left with an after-glow. A lot of the quality and nature of changa is dependent on the batch of ayahuasca vine that you use. We found quite early on that only with some batches of ayahuasca vine did we really obtain a warm afterglow, which does not occur so much with ayahuasca leaf.

I prefer to smoke changa in a joint, perhaps with two or three other people, outside in a special place sitting in nature. We pass it around and are silent for the most part, just experiencing this space together. Even groups of 12 people smoking a changa joint can be good, but passing around a pipe or bong can work just as well, and perhaps lead to stronger experiences.

When by oneself, a bong is probably the most efficient way to smoke changa, as it is perhaps the most efficient way to smoke DMT, wedged between layers of herb such as passionflower and taken down in one hit. Many explorers are now saying that a device called the 'vapor genie', a handheld vaporiser, is the most effective way to smoke changa – although I am personally yet to be convinced, and feel that the experience is a bit less immediate and direct than regular smoking methods.

I think smoking DMT once a day is far too often. Once a week is viable, once a month is fine too, but once every few months will ensure every ex-perience is special. Changa often works to align the system, and there will be a clearing, a mini-shift, that will occur. That being said, the shift could be very major! The plants do work on you, they operate on levels of the mind and beyond, and so you should feel much 'better' after smoking changa.

Changa should not be smoked with SSRI medication. DMT in any form does not tend to respond well to be being smoked by the alcoholically inebriated, with the resulting experiences often being very dark and disturbing. People should be very wary of smoking changa on MDMA, as there could be complex side effects, such as the potentially very dangerous 'serotonin syndrome'.

The second or third time you smoke changa in one session will normally be stronger because of the accumulation of the smoked harmine in the system. That being said, many experienced researchers do not feel that boosting the harmine content of changa is useful or necessary. The innovator of boosting harmine levels in changa is my friend 'Terrence McPhillip'. He first obtained 100 grams of ayahuasca leaves from me and made a 10X extract into 10 grams of ayahuasca leaves. Then he used this 10X extract to make changa. But he and his friends said the harmine imprint was too strong and too heavy! However, this information was shared with the Internet community and people began to make changa with a much stronger harmine imprint from ayahuasca leaf. The point is that harmine extracted from ayahuasca vine, rather than leaf, is as potent, if not more so. You do not need to boost the harmine levels in most batches of vine or vine leaf, as they are already strong enough to potentise the DMT in changa quite sufficiently. Higher harmine levels in changa have the same effect as higher harmine levels in ayahuasca brews: the experience tends to be heavier, more bodily-orientated and earthy.

Some people are putting extracted harmalas from Syrian rue in their changa, which can result in quite a harsh smoke, and according to some, a more scattered experience. A surprising number of people are not using ayahuasca vine or leaf at all, and in that case the experience does not last as long, there will be no afterglow, and the result will be a more cerebral, typical DMT-like experience, which is perhaps less integrated into the human framework.

Most people will respond very well to a light smoke of changa, and even though it can be a little intense, most people will appreciate its value. When starting by smoking small amounts, most people will not have a fearful or anxious experience. DMT is typically not as ego-shattering in the same way that other classic psychedelic compounds are, as for the most part, you retain your ego and simply expand your awareness.

In my view, changa is a very useful tool for opening up people to the existence of other realities. Many are using a 40 - 50% blend, which can equate to quite a strong DMT experience, yet it can be an incredibly paradigm-shattering experience. Once you go over that line, there is no turning back to the 'old paradigm', or at least, it will be very difficult to do so. However, at the end of the day, most people will be glad for that shift in their awareness. It is quite an initiation, and many will take to it like a duck to water.

How DMT shifts and assists people is not well studied. Having observed people taking DMT for 15 years, I can say there are shifts, and many people often do make quite significant changes in their lives, but it is not a wonder drug or some kind of ultimate panacea. People often report feeling more in touch with themselves, the universe and nature, and experience a felt sense of meaning in reality, which is then is revealed to be much more than structural and historical forms of mental or religious understanding. I think that changa is a good introduction to the tryptamines, but the experience is so short that ayahuasca is generally recommended to people who want to go deeper. The ayahuasca experience lasts four to six hours and allows much more work of all kinds to occur in the space.

For some people, changa is only recreational – and I personally don't see too much of a problem in that. The experience can certainly be very pleasant and presents less of a problem than smoking crystal DMT in larger amounts, when the experience can sometimes become quite 'dark'. Yet I think even purely recreational users generally treat it with respect. Some people will smell DMT on dancefloors at parties and assume their approach or attitude is casual or cavalier. However, if you talk to such people, they are usually quite experienced explorers who can actually handle being in this state among people in a state of celebration and oneness. Changa is rarely purely hedonistic in the way that most 'drugs' are for the majority of people. There is a level of intensity and consciousness expansion that meth or heroin users, for example, are just not seeking, or wanting. Almost all those who use changa recognise, or eventually come to recognise, its special and even 'sacred' nature.

I believe the potential for abuse with changa is relatively low. That is because it simply stops giving you the experiences you want to get from it if you try and squeeze too much out of it. There are very few difficulties or problems that people may run into via smoking changa, at least that I have heard of. One initial self appointed beta tester pretty much smoked non-stop all day, every day, for weeks and ran into no complications. Yet he is the only person I have ever heard of who has done this, and about the only person I know who has continued to gain value from continually smoking changa.

I believe changa is a very useful tool and feel very privileged to have been able to bring this revolutionary plant alchemy to the world. The biggest obstacle which prevents this technology of transformation getting to more people is its legal status, as crystal DMT is specifically scheduled as an illegal compound in almost every country in the world.

Bibliography

Alexander, Peter. *In the Land of the Mad King – Protocols of a New Medicine.* Self Published.

Badiner, Allan Hunt. *Zig Zag Zen.* Chronicle Books, April 1, 2002.

Brennan, Barbara Ann. *Hands of Light, Light Emerging.* Bantam, First Printing edition, November 1, 1993.

Callaway JC, McKenna DJ, Grob CS. *The Scientific Investigation of Ayahuasca: A Review of Past and Current Research.* The Heffter Review of Psychedelic Research, Volume 1, 1998.

Dolmatoff, Rachel. *Rainforest Shamans: Essays on the Tukano Indians of the Northwest Amazon.* Themis Books, April 1997.

Dostoyevsky, Fyodor. *Notes from the Underground.* Vintage Reprint edition, August 30, 1994.

Durckheim, Graf Karlfried. Hara: *The Vital Centre of Man.* Unwin Paperbacks, April 1988.

Eliade, Mircea. *Shamanism: Archaic Techniques of Ecstasy.* Translated: W.R. Trask. London: Routledge and Kegan Paul, 1964.

Friedman S., Metlin S., Svedi A. & Wender I., *Selective Hydrogenation of Polynuclear Aromatic Hydrocarbon.* J. Org. Chem., 1959, 24 (9), pp 1287–1289.

Gaup, Ailo. *The Shamanic Zone.* The Three Bears Company, 2005.

Gershon, Michael. *The Second Brain: A Groundbreaking New Understanding of Nervous Disorders of the Stomach and Intestine.* Harper Perennial, November 17, 1999.

Goodrick-Clarke, Clare. *Alchemical Medicine for the 21st Century: Spagyrics for Detox, Healing, and Longevity.* Healing Arts Press, June 8, 2010.

Grof, Stan with Christina Grof. *Spiritual Emergency: When Personal Transformation Becomes a Crisis.* Tarcher, 1st edition, September 1, 1989.

Grof, Stan. *The Cosmic Game: Explorations Of The Frontiers Of Human Consciousness* (1998). State University of New York Press, March 17, 2010.

Hancock, Graham. *Supernatural.* Disinformation Books, Revised edition, September 1, 2006.

Hofmann, Albert. *My Problem Child.* MAPS.org, 4th edition, March 1, 2009. http://www.maps.org/books/mpc/

Houston, Jean. *A Mythic Life.* Harper San Francisco, October 11, 1996.

Huxley, Aldous. *The Doors of Perception and Heaven and Hell.* 1954, 1956, Harper & Brothers.

Isherwood, Christopher. *Ramakrishna and his Disciples.* Shepheard-Walwyn, 1986.

Jansen, Karl. Ketamine: *Dreams and Realities.* MAPS, December 1, 2004. http://www.maps.org/books/K-DreamsKJansenMAPS.pdf

Jung, C.J. Memories, *Dreams and Reflections.* Vintage, April 23, 1989.

Krishnamurti, Jiddu. *Total Freedom: The Essential Krishnamurti.* HarperOne, June 2003.

Lahood, G.A. *Relational spirituality, Part 1. Paradise unbound: Cosmic hybridity and spiritual narcissism in the "one truth" of New Age transpersonalism.* International Journal of Transpersonal Studies,*29(1), 31-57, 2010.*

Leary, Timothy/ Metzner, Ralph/ Alpert, Richard, *The Psychedelic Experience: A Manual Based on the Tibetan Book of the Dead.* Citadel, October 1, 2000.

Lessing, Dorris. *The Golden Notebook.* Fourth Estate edition, January 30, 2012.

Lily, John. *The Scientist.* Ronin Publishing, 3rd edition, October 23, 1996.

Laing, R.D. *The Divided Self: An Existential Study in Sanity and Madness.* Harmondsworth, Penguin.

Laing, R.D. *The Politics of Experience and the Bird of Paradise.* Harmondsworth, Penguin.

Lowen, Alexander. *Betrayal of The Body.* The Alexander Lowen Foundation, February 1, 2012.

Maharshi, Ramana. *Talks with Ramana Maharshi: On Realizing Abiding Peace and Happiness.* Inner Directions, 2nd edition, July 1, 2000.

Masters, Robert Augustus. *Spiritual Bypassing: When Spirituality Disconnects Us from what Really Matters*. North Atlantic Books, July 27, 2010.

McKenna, Terence. *Food of the Gods: The Search for the Original Tree of Knowledge – A Radical History of Plants, Drugs, and Human Evolution*. New York: Bantam. 1992.

McKenna, Terence. *Numerous Talks*. https://archive.org/details/PsychedeliaRawArchivesOfTerenceMckennaTalks

Monroe, Robert. *Journeys Out of the Body*. 1st ed, Garden City, Doubleday, 1971

Monroe, Robert. *Far Journeys*. 1st ed, Garden City, Doubleday, 1985.

Müller-Ebeling, Claudia and Christian Rätsch and Surendra Bahadur Shahi (2002). *Shamanism and Tantra in the Himalayas*. Translated by Annabel Lee. Inner Traditions, September 1, 2002.

Oroc, James. *Tryptamine Palace 5-MeO-DMT and the Sonoran Desert Toad*. Park Street Press, 2009.

Ott, Jonathon. *Ayahuasca Analogues: Pangaean Entheogens*. Jonathan Ott Books, First edition, June 1994.

Ott, Jonathon. *Pharmacotheon: Entheogenic Drugs Their Plant Sources and Histories*. Jonathan Ott Books, 1st edition, February 1993.

Talks with Sri Nisargadatta, *I Am That*. Transcribed and edited by Maurice Frydman, Chetana Publishing, Bombay, 1973.

A.F. Price and Wong Translate, *The Diamond Sutra and The Sutra of Hui Neng*. Mou-Lam, Shambhala Publications, 1985.

Pierakkos, John. *Core Energetics: Developing the Capacity to Love And Heal*. Core Evolution Publishing; 2nd edition, December 30, 2005.

Saunders, Nicholas. *E for Ecstasy*. Self Published, First edition, April 26, 1993

Schwarz M.J., Houghton P.J., Rose S., Jenner P., Lees A.D. (2003) *Activities of extract and constituents of Banisteriopsis caapi relevant to parkinsonism*. Pharmacology, Biochemistry and Behavior, 75: 627-633.

Shannon, Benny. *Antipodes of The Mind*. Oxford University Press, USA, January 2, 2003.

Shannon, Benny. *The Epistemics of Ayahuasca Visions*. Phenomenology and the Cognitive Sciences, 9 (2):263-280, 2010.

Stoleroff, Myron. *From Thanatos To Eros*. Thaneros Press, October 1994. http://www.maps.org/t2e/

Strassman, Rick Slawek Wojtowicz, Luis Eduardo Luna and Ede Frecska. *Inner Paths to Outer Space: Journeys to Alien Worlds through Psychedelics and Other Spiritual Technologies*. Park Street Press, 2008.

Strassman, Rick , DMT: *The Spirit Molecule: A Doctor's Revolutionary Research into the Biology of Near-Death and Mystical Experiences*. Park Street Press, 2001.

Razam, Rak. *Aya Awakenings: A Shamanic Odyssey*. North Atlantic Books, November 5, 2013.

Reid, Daniel. *The Tao of Health, Sex, and Longevity: A Modern Practical Guide to the Ancient Way*. Fireside Books, July 15, 1989.

Robert, Jane. *Seth Speaks: The Eternal Validity of the Soul*. Amber-Allen Publishing, April 27, 2012.

Stevens, Jay. *Storming Heaven: LSD and the American Dream*. Grove Press, 1998.

Trungpa, Chogyam. *Cutting through Spiritual Materialism*. Shambhala Publications, September 28, 2010.

Turner, D.M. *A Psychedelic Guide*. Panther Press, September 1994. http://www.erowid.org/library/books_online/essential_psychedelic_guide/ essential_psychedelic_guide.shtml

Voogelbreinder, Snu. *Garden of Eden*. Self Published, 2009 1st edition.

Watts, Alan. 1958 *Nature, Man, and Woman*. Vintage, 1991.

Watts, Alan. 1966 *The Book: On the Taboo Against Knowing Who You Are*. Vintage reissue, 1989.

Wilber, Ken. *Sex, Ecology, Spirituality*. Shambhala Publications, 2000.

Wilber, Ken. *The Atman Project: A Transpersonal View of Human Development*. Shambhala Publications, 1980.

Wilson, Edward O. *Consilience*. Vintage Reprint edition, March 30, 1999.

Wolfe, Tom. *The Electric Kool Acid Test*. Picador, Sixth Printing edition, August 19, 2008.204204

Printed in November 2021
by Rotomail Italia S.p.A., Vignate (MI) - Italy